An Agenda for Development

Boutros Boutros-Ghali
Secretary-General of the United Nations

An Agenda
for Development
1995

With related UN documents

United Nations • New York, 1995

Department of Public Information

Office of Conference and Support Services
Department of Administration and Management

Editor's note:
Section One of this publication contains three reports on an Agenda for
Development prepared by the Secretary-General in response to a request by the
General Assembly. Section Two contains additional United Nations documents
reflecting the ongoing debate on this subject. In the symbols used for documents
referred to or reproduced in this publication, the letter "A" (e.g. A/48/935) indicates
a document of the General Assembly.

United Nations Publication
Sales No.E.95.I.16
ISBN 92-1-100556-6

**Published by the Department of Public Information
New York, NY 10017**

CONTENTS

Preface

1   D<small>EVELOPMENT</small> is the most important task facing humanity today. Yet, as the United Nations celebrates its fiftieth anniversary, we are in danger of losing sight of such an essential task. Beset by the growth of conflicts, and the necessity to maintain the peace in the tense post-cold war environment, we risk getting lost in the urgency of peace-keeping, at the expense of the longer term development effort.

2   In the last three years, the United Nations has started a process of re-examination and redefinition of development. Taking into account the progress achieved in the last half-century, we are engaged in a process aiming at nothing less than restoring to development questions the urgency they deserve.

3   Through a cycle of World Conferences, we are shaping a consensus around certain essential development values. At Rio de Janeiro, in 1992, the United Nations gathered the world community to discuss the links between environment and development. At Vienna, in 1993, the United Nations brought together world leaders, and representatives of civil society, to debate the proposition that, without full respect for human rights, there can be no lasting development. Indeed, at that Conference, the right to development was reaffirmed as a basic human right.

4   At Cairo, in 1994, the United Nations Conference on Population and Development re-established the population dimension as a central aspect of development. Population growth can be an asset to development, but unchecked growth in population can also represent a special challenge to the development effort.

5   In March 1995, at Copenhagen, the United Nations is organizing a World Summit for Social Development. At this Summit, age-old problems, such as poverty, unemployment and social dislocation, will be examined by the representatives of the world community. Renewed commitments will be made towards the eradication of poverty, imaginative approaches to the issues of unemployment will be presented and courageous initiatives to end social dislocation will be discussed.

6   In September 1995, at Beijing, the world community will gather, at the invitation of the United Nations, to discuss the integration of women in the development effort. Without the active participation of women, there can be no development. A greater role for women is both an indicator of development and a precondition for the development process to take place.

7   Finally, in 1996, at Istanbul, the World Conference on Human Settlements, Habitat II, is to be convened. The importance of this Conference, dealing with the many issues of development in an urban environment, is such that it has been rightly labelled "The City Summit".

8   Thus, as this century draws to a close, the United Nations is laying the foundations of a new consensus on development. An Agenda for Development is being written at these conferences of the United Nations. Member States are represented at those conferences at the highest level. In parallel, the input of non-governmental organizations, grassroots organizations and other representatives of civil society ensure that the programmes of action adopted at these conferences are based on a close reading of the needs of populations everywhere. Development, though requiring international cooperation, is the responsibility of Member States, but it can only succeed if it responds to the needs of the people, and if it articulates these needs into a coherent policy framework.

9   In the context of the preparation of an Agenda for Development, the General Assembly asked me to issue a report and recommendations as a contribution to the debate. I am therefore offering this collection of documents as a contribution to the process, continuing in the General Assembly, and in the Global Conference cycle of the United Nations, in the hope that this contribution will prove to be of some use in the finalization of an Agenda for Development.

10   The coming century should be the development century.

Section One
AN AGENDA
FOR DEVELOPMENT

The need for an Agenda

Progress in the implementation of
General Assembly resolution 47/181
Note by the Secretary-General
A/48/689, 29 November 1993

I. Introduction

1　THE PURPOSE of the present note is to provide information on progress in the implementation of General Assembly resolution 47/181 of 22 December 1992, in which the Assembly requested the Secretary-General, in consultation with Member States, to prepare an agenda for development for submission to it at its forty-eighth session.

2　Accordingly, the note provides information on the replies received from Member States in response to the Secretary-General's note verbale of 20 May 1993, eliciting views on an Agenda for Development. It also contains initial indications, in the light of these replies, as well as consultations within the Secretariat and with the organizations of the United Nations system, including at the recent session of the Administrative Committee on Coordination on 28 and 29 October 1993, as to some of the approaches and broad themes which the Secretary-General would propose to pursue in an Agenda for Development. It is hoped that this information will facilitate an open and wide-ranging debate in the meetings of the current session of the General Assembly to be devoted to this subject. The views expressed in the debate will be drawn upon in pursuing ongoing work in the preparation of the report on an Agenda for Development requested by the Assembly.

3　As far as the timetable for the issuance of the report is concerned, in the note verbale referred to above, the Secretary-General indicated that the complexity of the issues to be addressed in an Agenda for Development required a longer time-frame for its elaboration than that envisaged in General Assembly resolution 47/181.

This view was generally shared by Member States in their replies to
the note verbale. It is therefore the intention of the Secretary-General
to issue the report requested in General Assembly resolution 47/181
in the early months of 1994. In that light, it is proposed, for the
Assembly's consideration, that an item on the subject be included in
the agendas of the Economic and Social Council in 1994 and of the
forty-ninth session of the Assembly.

II. Replies received from Member States

4   As at 16 November 1993, the following Member States had
responded to the Secretary-General's note verbale of 20 May 1993:
Austria, Bangladesh, Brazil, Canada, China, Cuba, Denmark (on
behalf of the European Community), Finland (on behalf of the
Nordic countries), Ghana, Japan, Mexico, Morocco, Panama, Poland,
United Kingdom of Great Britain and Northern Ireland, United States
of America and Zimbabwe.

5   Many of the replies refer to peace and development as the
major twin themes of international cooperation. They note the opportunity provided by an Agenda for Development to redress what is
seen as a risk of marginalization of the United Nations system in the
economic and social sphere, and of a widening gap between the
objectives set out in an Agenda for Peace and the ability of the system
to advance the goals of sustained and sustainable development.

6   An overriding objective of an Agenda for Development
should thus be, in the view of many respondents, the enhancement of
international cooperation for the sustained growth of the world economy and, in particular, the revitalization of growth and development
of the developing countries.

7   Many replies state that an Agenda for Development should
address the root causes of instability, which are often directly linked
to poverty and underdevelopment. At the same time, the view is
expressed that, despite its indisputable links with peace, security and
stability, an agenda for development to overcome poverty and social

exclusion and enhance the well-being of people deserves to be dealt with in its own right. While the importance of human rights and democratization are generally recognized, different views are expressed, and emphasis placed, on their relationship with economic and social development.

8   Most responses agree that an Agenda for Development (a) should be an instrument for integrating new areas of consensus for action into an overall framework, drawing on relevant intergovernmental agreements, declarations and programmes of action, and (b) should provide a substantive basis to strengthen coordination of activities within the United Nations system.

A. *Agenda for Development as an instrument for integrating new areas of consensus*

9   Replies point to far-reaching changes taking place and trends emerging, which make it imperative for the international community to give renewed attention to the definition of development as a global issue and its place in the international agenda, and to review and reassess approaches to development at all levels.

10   In the same context, replies point to the growing globalization of the world economy and the increasing evidence of interdependence among countries and issues in the economic, social and environmental fields. They also highlight the gravity of the problems facing developing countries as well as the close interrelationships between sustained and sustainable development.

11   In the face of these changes and trends, areas of growing consensus are emerging. In this connection, replies highlight the integrative approach to ecological and economic issues developed at the United Nations Conference on Environment and Development. They also refer to the growing consensus around the concept of people-centred development, which guarantees equity and sustainability. Forthcoming conferences and summits on population, women and social development should serve to expand these areas of consensus.

12   Many respondents view the main potential contribution of an

Agenda for Development as helping to restore development cooperation as a central global concern, while promoting new, more comprehensive and effective approaches to development. It would do so by
building on objectives and commitments adopted in the General
Assembly and other international forums, assessing progress
achieved and proposing ways and means of overcoming obstacles
encountered, furthering emerging new areas of international consensus, and integrating them in the international framework.

13   The hope is expressed in many replies that, as part of a
process of renewal and consensus building, an Agenda for
Development should promote new partnerships among Governments,
based on the recognition of sovereign equality, mutual interest and
shared responsibility, as well as between Governments, the United
Nations and other actors in development. In this connection, a further
expansion of the development dialogue to include community organizations and non-governmental organizations, at both the national
and international levels, is seen as increasingly essential to arrive at
sound development strategies, based on popular participation and the
needs of the people.

14   Replies propose various priority objectives to be addressed.
Among them:

(a) Mobilizing new and additional financial resources, tak-
     ing into account, *inter alia*, the light of the urgent needs
     of the least developed countries, as well as of the
     economies in transition;

(b) Promoting the fulfilment of commitments in the areas of
     trade, money and finance and macroeconomic policy
     coordination, and ensuring fuller participation of devel-
     oping countries in international economic cooperation;

(c) Emphasizing investments in people;

(d) Advancing economic growth to foster long-term social
     progress, including income distribution;

(e) Alleviating demographic pressures;

(f) Promoting the participation of women in development.

B. *Agenda for Development as an instrument for enhancing coordination within the United Nations system*

15 Noting that the economic and social sectors of the United Nations suffer from an unclear identity, insufficient visibility and credibility, and excessive fragmentation, a number of replies see an Agenda for Development as an important vehicle for better defining the purposes, goals and role of the United Nations in development, in a way which would enhance both the effectiveness of its own interventions and its ability to develop well-defined positions contributing to improved coordination within the United Nations system as a whole.

16 Some countries draw attention to what they see as the three main functions of the United Nations:

   (a) A universal meeting place where all Members can raise issues for discussion and, hopefully, resolution;

   (b) An instrument for analysis and information gathering and for the elaboration of and monitoring of adherence to international norms;

   (c) A network of institutions entrusted with development as well as relief tasks in support of Member States.

17 Some replies also provide suggestions as to specific areas on which United Nations activities should focus. Among them:

   (a) Introducing strengthened mechanisms for macroeconomic policy surveillance and monitoring;

   (b) Overseeing issues relating to trade investments and commodities, including technology transfers and the fostering of greater technological cooperation among countries; addressing the emergence of new trade relationships, including trade-blocs and their impact on international trade;

   (c) Helping reconcile market-oriented approaches to development with social protection, welfare and equity considerations;

   (d) Addressing the role of foreign direct investments and transnational corporations in development;

(e) Advancing the sustainable development agenda;
(f) Assisting countries emerging from crisis situations in the rehabilitation phase and in setting their development agendas;
(g) Playing an advocacy role in the area of human capacity-building and furthering human resource development in developing countries, including as a means for their effective participation in international economic and trade relations;
(h) Building-up global databases in support of enhanced policy planning capacities in developing countries.

18 Replies reflect the expectation that, by promoting a more comprehensive and effective approach to development and a refocusing of the United Nations role and contribution, an Agenda for Development will, in turn, further the objective of greater coherence in the development activities of the system as a whole. Relationships, and the fostering of closer cooperation, between the United Nations and the Bretton Woods institutions are highlighted in many replies as a key issue in this respect. In the same context, the role of the multilateral financial institutions in mobilizing resources for use in social development projects is stressed. The need for improved coordination in the work of agencies concerned, respectively, with development financing and environmental issues is likewise highlighted.

19 In general, the fostering of a greater "unity of purpose" within the United Nations and the system as a whole, in both the policy and operational spheres, is viewed as a crucial objective of an Agenda for Development.

III. Some approaches and themes to be pursued in an Agenda for Development

20 In the light of the views put forward by Member States in different forums, and in response to the Secretary-General's note verbale, and taking into account ongoing discussions with programmes and agencies of the United Nations system, the Secretary-General wishes to offer some initial reflections on possible approaches to an Agenda for Development, and on some of the broad themes to be addressed in that report.

21 An Agenda for Development should not attempt to provide a new macroeconomic theory or seek to present an exhaustive analysis of the world economy. The most useful contribution which, in the Secretary-General's view, can be made at this stage through that report is to offer the international community an open working Agenda, which would be the beginning of a process rather than its end. In this perspective, its effectiveness should be judged, in the first instance, by the quality of the debate it generates and the follow-up given to it, through a process of discussion and consensus building, and the testing of new approaches.

22 In the post-colonial period, much of the impetus for development cooperation came from the bipolar competition. Today, that rationale has gone. The evidence, so far, is that the imperative of human solidarity does not have the mobilizing power of the cold war. Development appears to be slipping down the international agenda and risks to be increasingly marginalized in the face of short-term imperatives. An Agenda for Development should seek a reversal of these trends at all levels and help restore development to its rightful place at the top of the world agenda.

23 Economic growth is the mainspring of development. An acceleration of the rate of growth is a condition for expanding the resource base of the developing countries, and hence for economic, technological and social transformation.

24 In the continuum of the work of the United Nations for peace and development, preventive diplomacy seeks to avoid the breakdown of conditions of peace. At the other end of the continuum, post-conflict peace-building must involve efforts to identify and support structures which build trust and well-being among peoples. The promotion of economic and social development is crucial at both ends of the continuum.

25 Traditional approaches to development have failed to trans-

form poor countries and countries in post-conflict situations. They have not succeeded in achieving growth in most developing countries and, more importantly, have failed to reduce poverty and to set the stage for sustainable progress. The assumption of conditions of peace, on which development strategies have traditionally been built, is in stark contrast with the actual situation prevailing in a growing number of countries in Africa, as well as elsewhere.

26   An Agenda for Development would thus complement an Agenda for Peace, by addressing the deeper foundations of global peace and security in the economic, social and environmental spheres.

27   One of the contributions of an Agenda for Development should be to bring out the new face of the world economy, stressing the globalization of economic flows, and taking stock of the increased interdependence among nations and issues.

28   Greater interdependence among nations, facilitated by liberalization and deregulation and driven by technological innovation, means that economic problems must, now more than ever before, be seen in a global perspective. The distinction between national and international economic policies is fading. Financial and trade flows and international cooperation in the area of technology need to be re-examined in this context.

29   Growing levels of interdependence also require a rethinking of the overall content of development cooperation. It is frequently equated with the concessional elements injected into the trade, finance and technology flows between developed and developing countries. These elements remain important. In this context, the consequences and impact of a premature reduction in the availability of official development assistance should not be underestimated. For many developing countries, however, trade, debt and private flows are equally, if not more, crucial. Development cooperation today must mean the integration of developing countries' concerns into all discussions of global trade, finance and technology cooperation.

30   During the past decade, only a few developing countries have been successful in expanding their exports and achieving self-

reliance. For most of them, the full potential for enhancing export earnings through gains from trade liberalization has not yet been realized. Protectionism is still high and reduces the capacity of developing countries to generate additional financial resources for development through higher export earnings. A major factor inhibiting investment in export supply capabilities is uncertainty as to whether current access levels will be liberalized, curtailed or remain unchanged.

31 Technology, whether embodied in physical capital or in the knowledge processed by human beings, is a powerful engine for growth. Technology is also fundamental and the key element in the process of globalization. A sustained development process will not take place unless countries participate in the progress made possible by the rapid advances in science and technology that have characterized the global economy in recent years and will continue in the future. Technology has to be developed, deployed and shared, not just for promoting growth, but also for environmental management and poverty alleviation. Access to technology will be one of the determining factors for growth in the world economy. As the world becomes increasingly integrated, the comparative advantage of all nations is likely to rest on the skill, education and technical competence of their labour force.

32 Development must thus be seen as a shared concern of all nations, rich and poor, whatever their orientations. In addressing development as a key global issue, commonalities as well as the specificity of conditions and requirements must be fully borne in mind. One important commonality relates to the place of developing countries in the international economic system and their capacity to affect decisions which have sometimes a profound impact on opportunities for their economic and social development. There are, at the same time, specificities which must be clarified and addressed, if development support actions are to have the necessary impact and meet the specific requirements of the countries concerned.

33 An important illustration in this respect is the particular problems being faced by countries in transition. This situation is common to a large number of countries, not only in Eastern Europe but also in Africa, Asia and Latin America, where the move to a more market-oriented system is being undertaken, with all the promise, but also all the difficulties, which this process implies.

34   A second illustration relates to the requirements of countries emerging from natural disasters. No geographical area is exempt. The challenge of effective international relief in such situations and of proceeding from relief to rehabilitation and the resumption of development will need to be addressed in an Agenda for Development.

35   A third example relates to the support requirements of countries which are in the midst of a conflict, be it the result of a civil war or an international conflict. The challenge of pursuing development efforts in such situations is a reality with which the United Nations is increasingly faced and which will have to be taken into account in an Agenda for Development.

36   A fourth illustration relates to the requirements of countries which are recovering from a conflict. Their special development needs are also not accounted for in traditional development theory and will need to be brought out in an Agenda for Development.

37   The need to pursue a more holistic view of development, fully encompassing economic as well as social dimensions, and the importance of taking into account the specificities of particular requirements and situations, should not preclude the identification of areas of concentration and priority themes for United Nations actions. Ways of enhancing the role of the General Assembly and the Economic and Social Council in promoting policy development at the national and regional levels and harmonizing policies at the international level in relation to these themes will need to be examined. The contribution of special conferences should be reviewed in the same context.

38   An assessment of development assistance policies and of the role of the United Nations in supporting the development of national capacities should, equally, form an important part of this debate, as should the contribution of the United Nations in promoting the role of the private sector and the development of entrepreneurship.

39 The search for more effective approaches to development and a sharpening of the role of the United Nations in development, should, in turn, provide the basis for an examination of ways of enhancing inter-agency coordination, including closer cooperation with the Bretton Woods institutions. In the same perspective, an Agenda for Development should include a discussion of the regional dimension of development, including the role of the regional commissions and relations with regional organizations outside the United Nations system.

40 The title of the report which the Secretary-General is to submit to the General Assembly will be *An Agenda for Development*. The use of the indefinite article is significant. The contribution of each and every State, in the further elaboration of the Agenda will be vital. The presentation by the Secretary-General of an "open", "working" Agenda should be the beginning of a new process of dialogue where all States can contribute to the determination of their common future, and it should serve to generate a renewed debate among Member States as to the development themes and priorities to be addressed by the United Nations. This should, in turn, lead to a new sense of cohesion among all parts of the system.

41 The Secretary-General invites the views of the Member States on this approach.

An Agenda for Development

Report of the Secretary-General
A/48/935, 6 May 1994

Preface

1   THE GENERAL ASSEMBLY, in its resolution 47/181 of 22 December 1992, requested me to submit, in consultation with Member States, a report on an agenda for development. In an effort to gather the widest range of views about the topic of development, I asked for submissions from all Member States, as well as the agencies and programmes of the United Nations system, and encouraged ideas from public and private sources on a worldwide basis. Contributions received in the course of this process have been drawn upon in preparing the present report.

2   As requested in paragraph 5 of General Assembly resolution 48/166 of 21 December 1993, I will present my conclusions and recommendations on an agenda for development during the forty-ninth session of the Assembly, taking into account the debate at the substantive session of 1994 of the Economic and Social Council, as well as the views expressed during the discussions to be promoted by the President of the General Assembly.

I. Introduction: why an Agenda for Development?

3   Development is a fundamental human right. Development is the most secure basis for peace.

4   Taking stock of these principles, and in keeping with my strong personal commitment to development and the recognized needs of the United Nations at this point in history, the idea of an agenda for development took shape.

5   The concept of development, and decades of effort to reduce poverty, illiteracy, disease and mortality rates, are great achievements of this century. But development as a common cause is in danger of fading from the forefront of our agenda. The competition for influence during the cold war stimulated interest in development. The motives were not always altruistic, but countries seeking to develop could benefit from that interest. Today, the competition to bring development to the poorest countries has ended. Many donors have grown weary of the task. Many of the poor are dispirited. Development is in crisis.

   6   The poorest nations fall farther behind. Nations in transition from command to open economies face immense hardships. Nations that have achieved prosperity see their success accompanied by a new array of problems, social, environmental, cultural and economic, and many are consequently reluctant even to pursue their assistance policies at former levels.

   7   The current situation calls for wider intellectual understanding, deeper moral commitment and more effective policy measures. Without them, a half century of considerable progress could be undermined. Worse, all peoples of the world will live on a deteriorating planet, and will increasingly lose the ability to shape their destiny in a coherent way.

   8   Specific suggestions and detailed proposals for development have been produced in great quantity and are deserving of serious study. The United Nations system has produced a wealth of studies and reports on various aspects of development; they are an invaluable resource.

   9   Building upon these efforts, the present report seeks to revitalize the vision of development and to stimulate an intensified discussion of all its aspects.

   10   The Charter of the United Nations makes possible a maturing elaboration of the crucial idea of development, but it has been left to us in the last decades of the twentieth century to try to bring the concept of development to fulfilment.

   11   Concerns have been expressed that the United Nations puts greater emphasis on peace-keeping than on issues of development.

These fears are not borne out by the regular budgets or the numbers of staff members engaged in peace and in development. Yet with growing requests for funds for peace-keeping, some Member States find it difficult to increase their contributions to the developmental activities of the United Nations. Without development, however, there is no prospect for lasting peace.

12   While national Governments bear the major responsibility for development, the United Nations has been entrusted with important mandates for assisting in this task. The involvement of the United Nations in development spans five development decades and encompasses the full range of global problems of an economic, social, cultural and humanitarian character. It operates in all categories and at every level of development.

13   This agenda, therefore, is grounded in unique United Nations experience. Section II sets forth the five major and interlinked dimensions of development. Section III notes the multiplicity of actors in development and the process by which the United Nations can help to link these actors to the different dimensions of development. Annex I to the present report shows the scale of the United Nations involvement in development. In discussing the involvement of the United Nations in development, I have primarily limited myself to the United Nations itself, including its funds and programmes. The work of the specialized agencies of the United Nations system, essential as it is, is not the focus of the present document.

14   In the light of the new vision of development that is emerging, an alternative to the United Nations in development simply does not exist. The United Nations is a forum where the voices of all States, great and small, can be heard with equal clarity, and where non-State actors can make their views known to the widest audience. There is still time to move forward together, but greater urgency is necessary. With each passing day's delay, the work grows more costly and difficult.

15   While there is war, no State is securely at peace. While there is want, no people can achieve lasting development.

II. The dimensions of development

A. Peace as the foundation

16 Traditional approaches to development presuppose that it takes place under conditions of peace. Yet that is rarely the case. The absence of peace is a pervasive reality in many parts of the world. Most peoples must strive to achieve their development against a background of past, present or threatened conflict. Many carry the burden of recent devastation and continuing ethnic strife. None can avoid the realities of a world of ongoing arms proliferation, regional war, and the possibility of a return to potentially antagonistic spheres of influence. To the categorization of countries by level of development should be added the categorization of countries in conflict. Because the United Nations is active at the forefront of humanitarian aid, refugee assistance, and the range of peace operations, it is deeply and inextricably involved in peace as a fundamental dimension of development.

17 Development cannot proceed easily in societies where military concerns are at or near the centre of life. Societies whose economic effort is given in substantial part to military production inevitably diminish the prospects of their people for development. The absence of peace often leads societies to devote a higher percentage of their budget to the military than to development needs in health, education and housing. Preparation for war absorbs inordinate resources and impedes the development of social institutions.

18 The lack of development contributes to international tension and to a perceived need for military power. This in turn heightens tensions. Societies caught in this cycle find it difficult to avoid involvement in confrontation, conflict or all-out warfare.

19 While in some nations service in the military is the most reliable path to an education and to the acquisition of job skills for civilian life, there are also cases in which military production may disseminate advanced technologies of eventual use for civilian purposes. But national budgets which focus directly on development better serve the cause of peace and human security.

20   Situations of conflict require a development strategy different from that obtaining under peaceful conditions. The characteristics of development will differ according to the nature of the situation. Development in the context of international war does not involve the same problems as development during guerrilla warfare, or development when governmental institutions are under military control.

21   Although development activities yield their best results in conditions of peace, they should start prior to the end of hostilities. Emergency relief and development should not be regarded as alternatives; one provides a starting point and a foundation for the other. Relief requirements must be met in a way which, from the outset, provides a foundation for lasting development. Camps for refugees and displaced persons must be more than mere holding grounds for victims. Vaccination campaigns, literacy drives and special attention to the conditions of women are important at these times. All can lay the groundwork for community development even while emergency relief is being provided. Capacity-building steps should not await the formal termination of hostilities, but must begin to be performed alongside urgent wartime services. Conflict, terrible as it is, can provide opportunities for major reform and its consolidation. The ideals of democracy, respect for human rights and measures for social justice can begin to take form at this stage.

22   Peace-building means action to identify and support structures which will tend to strengthen and solidify peace in order to avoid a relapse into conflict. As preventive diplomacy aims to prevent the outbreak of a conflict, peace-building starts during the course of a conflict to prevent its recurrence. Only sustained, cooperative work on the underlying economic, social, cultural and humanitarian problems can place an achieved peace on a durable foundation. Unless there is reconstruction and development in the aftermath of conflict, there can be little expectation that peace will endure.

23   Peace-building is a matter for countries at all stages of development. For countries emerging from conflict, peace-building offers the chance to establish new institutions, social, political and judicial, that can give impetus to development. Land reform and other mea-

sures of social justice can be undertaken. Countries in transition can use peace-building measures as a chance to put their national systems on the path of sustainable development. Countries high on the scale of wealth and power must hasten the process of partial demobilization and defence conversion. Decisions made at this stage can have an immense impact on the course of their societies and the international community for future generations.

24   The most immediate task for peace-building is to alleviate the effects of war on the population. Food aid, support for health and hygiene systems, the clearance of mines and logistical support to essential organizations in the field represent the first peace-building task.

25   At this stage too, it is essential that efforts to address immediate needs are undertaken in ways that promote, rather than compromise, long-term development objectives. As food is provided there must be concentration on restoring food production capacities. In conjunction with the delivery of relief supplies, attention should be given to road construction, restoration and improvement of port facilities and establishment of regional stocks and distribution centres.

26   Mine clearance is a unique post-conflict undertaking. The world is awakening to the reality that the proliferation of land-mines poses a major obstacle to development and must be halted. Because they remain in the ground long after hostilities have ended, killing and maiming indiscriminately, mines effectively prevent the use of large tracts of land, while imposing a huge burden on families and the health infrastructures of post-conflict countries. In many cases, the removal of land-mines and unexploded ordnance is a prerequisite for all other post-conflict peace-building activities. Techniques applicable under conditions prevalent in most countries are slow and painstaking. Mine clearance has to be conducted for a great many years and therefore must be managed and undertaken by nationals. Capacity needs to be established to undertake, monitor and assess mine clearance and to maintain national standards in accordance with international guidelines.

27   The reintegration of combatants is difficult, but it is critically

important to stability in the post-conflict period. In many conflicts, soldiers have been recruited at a very young age. As a result, the capacity of former combatants to return to peacetime society and make a living is severely compromised, thereby undermining society's prospects for development.

28   Effective reintegration of combatants is also essential to the sustainability of peace. Credit and small-enterprise programmes are vital if ex-combatants are to find productive employment. Basic education for re-entry into civilian society, special vocational programmes, on-the-job training, and education in agricultural techniques and management skills are key to post-conflict peace-building. To a certain extent, some technical skills learned by soldiers can be important to national reconstruction.

29   As conflict typically takes a heavy toll on the mechanisms of governance, post-conflict efforts must pay special attention to their repair. Key institutions of civil society, judicial systems, for example, may need to be reinforced or even created anew. This means assistance for a variety of governmental activities, such as a fair system for generating public sector revenue, a legislative basis for the protection of human rights, and rules for the operation of private enterprise.

30   Pulling up the roots of conflict goes beyond immediate post-conflict requirements and the repair of war-torn societies. The underlying conditions that led to conflict must be addressed. As the causes of conflict are varied, so must be the means of addressing them. Peace-building means fostering a culture of peace. Land reform, water-sharing schemes, common economic enterprise zones, joint tourism projects and cultural exchanges can make a major difference. Restoring employment growth will be a strong inducement to the young to abandon the vocation of war.

31   Reduction of military expenditure is a vital link in the chain between development and peace. Although worldwide military expenditures continue to consume too large a share of productive resources and capacity, progress has been made in recent years. Worldwide, between 1987 and 1992 a cumulative peace dividend of

$500 billion was realized; $425 billion in industrial and transitional countries and $75 billion in developing countries. Little of this peace dividend appears to have been channelled into development.

32   While figures for exports of weapons show substantial declines in real terms in the early years of this decade, major concerns persist. Imported stocks of conventional weapons from countries rapidly reducing their military establishments are finding their way to third countries. Relatively unsophisticated weapons such as mortars, machine-guns and rocket launchers, even in the hands of those with rudimentary military training, have caused immense death and destruction. Paradoxically, those expressing great concern over the rising stocks of arms worldwide are also the source of that phenomenon. The five permanent members of the Security Council account for 86 per cent of the arms supplies now flowing to the countries of the world.

33   Imports of armaments are often purchased at the expense of capital or consumer goods. Reducing military expenditures makes more funds available to finance development, satisfy consumer demands and meet basic social welfare needs. A decrease in military outlays may support budgetary reform and promote macroeconomic stability. National efforts can be reoriented away from military priorities towards more productive and peaceful objectives. Global tensions and rivalries can be reduced. The overall impact on development is potentially profound.

34   The armed forces absorb some of the most talented members of society, whose training costs are considerably above the social average and whose energies are directed to the operation of increasingly sophisticated military hardware. Armament production utilizes industrial skills and capacity that could be put to other uses.

35   Among many of the countries in transition, procurement of new weapons systems has collapsed and most military expenditure is now for personnel costs, including pensions. Whole communities which were dependent on defence industries are now threatened, unless they can adapt themselves to changing requirements. Fears of further increases in unemployment are slowing reductions in the size

of armed forces, while military industries are being kept solvent by massive subsidies to the detriment of overall macroeconomic goals.

36 Demilitarization has also produced painful strains among the industrialized market economies, though less severe than those in countries in transition. Particular localities and firms have been severely affected, but the market mechanism has made it easier for resources to be absorbed in other sectors of the economy. Alternative employment has often been difficult to find for many workers however, and retraining remains sporadic.

37 These problems, however, should not deter countries from promoting the transition towards smaller militaries. The reduction of military spending not only frees up public expenditures for social purposes, but also allows credit to flow to needed economic investments. Over the longer term, these transitions will prove worthwhile, even if they are painful in the short term.

38 While it had been hoped that the end of the cold war would lead to a dramatic fall in military spending, progress has been difficult to achieve in an atmosphere increasingly marked by ethnic strife and economic insecurity. Relief at the end of the bipolar arms race is being supplanted by alarm over the prospect of several regional build-ups of both conventional arms and weapons of mass destruction. In a number of countries, especially in the Middle East and Asia, military expenditure has continued to increase. Fear of confrontation over shared resources, domestic instability and fear of heavily armed neighbours have all been factors. In some instances, the diminished possibility of super-Power intervention has increased the explosiveness of regional antagonisms. The lucrative aspects of the arms trade should also be taken into account. In this context, I support calls for a worldwide ban on the production and transfer of land-mines and their components.

39 Arms control and disarmament reduce the threat of destruction, economic decline and tensions that lead to war. A world of lower military expenditures, reduced military establishments, smaller stocks of weapons and less environmental destruction by military-related activities is not only desirable in itself, but propitious for development.

40   Today, even remote conflicts can pose security and developmental concerns far beyond a State's borders. This new recognition gives international peace and security a wider meaning, calls for measures that can further development even during conflict, and indicates that development, when successfully pursued, is another way to define peace.

B. *The economy as the engine of progress*

41   Economic growth is the engine of development as a whole. Without economic growth, there can be no sustained increase in household or government consumption, in private or public capital formation, in health, welfare and security levels. By whatever social processes distributional choices are made, the capacity to make them is severely limited in poor societies and is enhanced by economic growth. Progress in the other aspects of development discussed in this report, peace, the environment, society and democracy, will have a positive effect on economic growth.

42   Accelerating the rate of economic growth is a condition for expanding the resource base and hence for economic, technological and social transformation. While economic growth does not ensure that benefits will be equitably distributed or that the physical environment will be protected, without economic growth the material resources for tackling environmental degradation will not exist, nor will it be possible to pursue social programmes effectively in the long term. The advantage of economic growth is that it increases the range of human choice.

43   It is not sufficient, however, to pursue economic growth for its own sake. It is important that growth be sustained and sustainable. Growth should promote full employment and poverty reduction, and should seek improved patterns of income distribution through greater equality of opportunity.

44   If poverty persists or increases and there is neglect of the human condition, political and social strains will endanger stability over time. The reduction of poverty requires development in which access to the benefits of economic progress are as widely available as possible, and not concentrated excessively in certain localities, sectors or groups of the population.

45   Improved education, health and shelter, together with an increase in meaningful employment opportunities, will contribute directly to reducing poverty and its consequences. Apart from being desirable goals in themselves, education, health and shelter are all essential to a productive workforce and hence to economic growth. The elimination of hunger and malnutrition should be targets in their own right.

46   For sustained growth to take place, two conditions are necessary; a supportive national environment, and a favourable international climate. Without appropriate national policies, no amount of assistance, bilateral or multilateral, will lead to sustained growth. On the contrary, assistance given in this way can reinforce dependence on the outside world. Without a favourable international climate, domestic policy reform will be difficult to achieve, threatening the success of reforms and increasing the hardships suffered by the population.

47   Successful national economic experiences must be based on pragmatic policies. The need to take advantage of the efficiency of markets must be tempered by recognition of the need for Governments to act where markets cannot provide all the answers.

48   Governments can no longer be assumed to be paramount economic agents. They nevertheless retain the responsibility to provide a regulatory framework for the effective operation of a competitive market system. Governments have to intervene where appropriate: to invest in infrastructure, to facilitate the development of productive sectors, to provide an enabling environment for the promotion of private enterprise, to ensure that proper social safety nets are in place, to invest in human capital and to protect the environment. Governments provide the framework in which individuals can plan their long-term prospects.

49   There are no definite prescriptions for a division of roles. Public and private expenditures are not invariably substitutes for one another. The relationship between them is frequently of a complementary rather than a competitive character. Government policies for the promotion of a sound macroeconomic framework are essential for

sustained economic growth. Such macroeconomic policies, however, must rest upon solid micro-economic foundations which provide for the efficient allocation of scarce resources. Should markets fail to perform their functions, or fail to address essential welfare considerations, there is scope for government intervention. However, government policies and programmes are subject to failure as well; in such circumstances an empowered private sector can be essential.

50   Finding the right blend of government direction of the economy and encouragement of private initiative is perhaps the most pressing challenge of economic development. This is not only a problem for developing or transitional economies. In the search for the difficult path which lies between *dirigisme* and *laissez-faire,* all countries are involved. Major market economies, with recurrent recession and persistent high rates of unemployment, are also facing this challenge.

51   Increasing interdependence among nations has accelerated the transmission of both positive growth impulses and negative shocks. As a result, economic problems, even at the national level, now have to be seen in their global context. The distinction between national and international economic policies is fading. No nation, however successful, can insulate itself from the demographic, environmental, economic, social and military problems which exist in the world. The effects of deprivation, disease and strife in one part of the globe are felt everywhere. They will not be successfully managed until global development is under way.

52   All countries are part of an international economic system, but while many countries remain imperfectly integrated into it, others are excessively vulnerable to its instability. Development is hampered by external debt problems, the decrease in external resource flows, sharply declining terms of trade and mounting barriers to market access. Inadequate technological cooperation has prevented many countries from improving the efficiency of resource use, thus adversely affecting their international competitiveness and further inhibiting their integration into the world economy.

53   The expansion of international trade is essential to economic growth and is an integral part of the economic dimension of develop-

ment. The benefits of increased commerce and trade are not in doubt: lower transaction costs, greater economic opportunities and enhanced international confidence, trust and security.

54   Difficult access to the world trading system is an enormous obstacle to development. At present, that system often discriminates against the developing world by limiting its advantage in low labour costs, while the price of many primary commodities has tended to decline.

55   The internationalization of economic activity, the increasing reliance on market forces, the widespread recognition that private initiative is a potent force for economic growth, and the massive efforts undertaken towards trade liberalization by developing and transitional countries call for an open and transparent trading system in which rules and disciplines are respected by all. When countries find that they have a distinct comparative advantage in one particular economic activity and invest accordingly, they should not be confronted later with new protectionist measures when their investment is beginning to yield fruit and their product penetrates other markets.

56   But economic interdependence is rapidly becoming far more than a matter of trade and finance. There are also strong trends towards greater openness in the movement of funds, people and ideas around the world. This has encouraged Governments to create a national environment that attracts outside investment.

57   The pursuit of globally responsible macroeconomic policies by those countries whose economic strength shapes the international economic environment is essential to all development efforts. The role of the major economies in world finance remains preponderant. Their policies on interest rates, inflation and exchange rate stability are particularly significant. Exchange rate volatility compounds the debt problem through its effect on interest rates, foreign exchange earnings and reserves, and debt servicing. The policies the major economies follow in their domestic affairs will be of decisive importance in a world increasingly characterized by global capital markets.

58   Effective international cooperation for development cannot succeed unless the major economies make it their own objective. No

mechanism exists by which the major economies can be induced to make globally beneficial structural change in their own economies, or to adopt more globally responsible economic, fiscal and monetary policies.

59   At present, economic policy coordination among the major economies centres on the Group of Seven industrialized countries. Repeated efforts by the developing world, such as the current attempt to create a Group of Seven-Group of Fifteen (Summit Level Group for South-South Consultation and Cooperation) connection, have failed. With the recognition that growth in the major industrialized countries is no longer the sole engine of global development, change is warranted so that the processes of economic policy coordination become more broad-based.

60   The mechanisms for integrating responsible economic policies at the international level and growth at the national level are not yet fully developed. Leading the list of priorities are adequate measures to reduce the crippling burden of international debt, policies to discourage tendencies towards protectionism, and ensuring that the developing world shares in the benefits of the new World Trade Organization regime.

61   The lack of financial resources necessary for economic development is exacerbated by the debt crisis, which makes an already difficult situation much worse. In the last decade, indebted developing countries have had to transfer on average between 2 and 3 per cent of their gross domestic product (GDP) abroad; in some instances transfers have amounted to 6 per cent or more of GDP. Perversely, some developing countries have now become net exporters of financial resources.

62   The debt problem has many facets. Large amounts are owed to commercial banks by some countries. Many low-income countries owe large amounts to official bilateral and multilateral creditors. Efforts have been made to restructure commercial debt and, in certain cases, forgive bilateral official debt. But not enough has been done to alleviate the burden of multilateral debt or to assist countries that, despite a large debt-servicing burden, are not in default.

63   No single formula for generating economic growth exists,

but, half a century after the emergence of development as an independent field of inquiry, certain basic conditions are recognized as essential. Foremost among these is the need to take a strategic decision for development. The State must have the political will to act.

64 Development decisions are not taken in a vacuum. All societies must take into account previous development choices, political constituencies, structures of production, relations with the external environment and cultural values and expectations. The pattern of growth will depend to a large extent upon the influence of these factors and the compromises they entail.

65 The experience of countries which have achieved rapid development in the past few years can be seen as the outcome of a conscious choice by the State to give strategic priority to growth. The influence of State policies, for example in encouraging research and development or providing infrastructural and educational support, has been crucial. This does not mean, however, that growth takes place through State institutions. The State gives an impetus to growth; but it is the economy that needs to grow, not the State itself.

66 It is the State which must translate growth into forms acceptable to its political constituencies. Whatever the mode of production adopted, sustained growth which relies on the accumulation of capital, physical, human and institutional, will entail certain sacrifices of present consumption. The decision to defer consumption in favour of expected future returns is a political choice, as much as it is a decision by individuals to save.

67 The basic lesson of recent decades remains valid; as conditions, circumstances and capacities differ, so too must the mechanisms for generating growth. Growth requires political commitment and vision. The United Nations can act as facilitator and communicator, but it cannot substitute for the commitment of individual States and their domestic and international partners.

C. The environment as a basis for sustainability

68 The environment, like peace, the economy, society and

democracy, permeates all aspects of development, and has an impact on countries at all levels of development. In the developing world, ecological pressure threatens to undermine long-term development. Among many countries in transition, decades of disregard for the environment have left large areas poisoned and unable to sustain economic activity in the long term. Among the wealthiest nations, consumption patterns are depleting world resources in ways that jeopardize the future of world development.

69   Development and environment are not separate concepts, nor can one be successfully addressed without reference to the other. The environment is a resource for development. Its condition is an important measure and its preservation a constant concern of development. Successful development requires policies that incorporate environmental considerations. This link was accepted at the United Nations Conference on Environment and Development (UNCED) in 1992. That Conference provided a model for other efforts toward greater coherence in development.

70   Preserving the availability and rationalizing the use of the earth's natural resources are among the most compelling issues that individuals, societies and States must face. A country's natural resources are often its most easily accessible and exploitable development assets. How well these natural resources are managed and protected has a significant impact on development and on a society's potential for progress.

71   In the context of development, each society must confront the difficult challenges associated with protecting the long-term potential of its natural resources. Competing needs and interests must be balanced. Present social and economic needs must be satisfied in ways that do not undermine long-term resource availability, or the viability of the ecosystems on which we, and future generations, depend.

72   Environmental degradation reduces both the quality and the quantity of many resources used directly by people. The consequences of failing to pay adequate attention to natural resource destruction can be catastrophic. Water pollution damages fisheries. Increasing salinity and erosion of topsoil lowers crop yields.

Agricultural degradation and deforestation have promoted drought and soil erosion, and made malnutrition and famine increasingly familiar occurrences in certain regions. Overfishing and the exhaustion of marine resources have put ancient communities at risk. Excessive logging and the destruction of rain forests have destroyed important natural habitats, and undermined global biodiversity. Environmentally unsound practices in the extraction of natural resources have left large regions barren and contaminated.

73   Most alarming is the fact that degradation can, in some cases, be irreversible. Practices that will do permanent damage to the health of the planet should be urgently identified. Such practices must be halted.

74   While ensuring the preservation of natural resources implies certain limitations, it also provides many valuable incentives and opportunities for new thinking. Science and technology can play an important role. Increased energy efficiency and the development of new and renewable sources of energy will be essential. A change in lifestyles and attitudes towards energy consumption by more affluent people, along with more efficient production processes, will contribute to a more sustainable pattern of global development.

75   Integrating natural resource management and conservation into national development can have many broadly beneficial results. Tourism, upon which many countries rely, can bring important benefits, including vital infrastructure creation, increased direct and indirect employment, enhanced foreign exchange earnings, heightened environmental awareness, increased international exposure and unique opportunities for building a stronger national identity. It is important to develop sustainable tourism strategies which preserve the natural environment.

76   Initiatives now being pioneered in several Member States are also demonstrating the importance of community involvement in all development efforts. By making local inhabitants incentive partners rather than simply collateral beneficiaries, these programmes have broken new ground. The results in many places have been significant, leading to increased appreciation for the benefits of preserving natural resources, greater community cooperation in preserving tourist

assets and higher rural incomes. They are important examples from which many others can learn and benefit.

77   The link between the environment and development involves much more than the sound exploitation of natural resources however. Preserving and protecting the ecological equilibrium of our environment is a vital component not only of human development, but also of human survival.

78   Social welfare is reduced by ill health and premature mortality caused by degradation of air and water quality and by other environmental risks. Pollutants can cause health problems through direct exposure, or indirectly through changes in the physical environment. Threats to health range from increased exposure to ultraviolet radiation to deterioration in food and water quality.

79   Toxic chemicals and heavy metals can contaminate rivers and other water supplies. Many of these contaminants can be hard to remove from drinking water using standard purification techniques. Pollutants can be absorbed by people who do not realize that the food is contaminated. The exposure to hazardous materials and the risk of contamination as a result of industrial accidents are also issues linking environment and development.

80   Although discussion of the tangible and material aspects of the environment often eclipses discussion of other benefits, the intrinsic worth and value of nature itself should be respected and the intangible satisfaction that can be derived from enjoying the natural environment should be recognized.

81   Natural disasters can have an enormous and dramatic impact on development efforts. Because natural disasters can quickly devour hard-won achievements, planning must focus on ways to cushion the inevitable shocks, so that social structures will not be irreparably damaged, economic initiatives will not be forever set back, and natural disaster victims will not be condemned to perpetual dependence on external assistance.

82   Improved environmental management requires that businesses, households, farmers, the international community and Governments change the way they behave. Targeted policies are needed to ensure that

environmental values are properly reflected in economic activity. Public as well as private enterprises must be held accountable for the environmental impact of their activities, and Governments must take the lead in formulating policies and pursuing development strategies that encourage environmentally sound development.

83 In many countries, institutional inadequacies are proving to be major obstacles to the design and implementation of environmentally sound and responsible development projects. Therefore, national capacities for designing, implementing and enforcing environmental policies must be strengthened.

84 The interconnections between the environment, society, the economy and political participation highlight the importance of addressing the environmental aspect of development in a national context. The link between poverty and environmental sustainability is particularly compelling. Although poor communities often have a strong ethic of stewardship in managing their traditional lands, growing population pressures and a lack of resources often make it difficult for them to avoid degrading their environment. The very poor, struggling at the edge of subsistence, are preoccupied with day-to-day survival. Often, they are both victims and agents of environmental deterioration. Policies that improve the environment, reducing water contamination, for example, often bring the greatest positive benefit to the poorest members of society. Policies that are effective in reducing poverty will help reduce population growth and decrease pressure on the environment.

85 Policies that promote technological cooperation and the efficient use of resources can also help in finding solutions to environmental challenges. The relationships between inputs and outputs and the overall effects of economic activity on the environment are continually changing. The key to increased sustainability is not necessarily to produce less, but rather to produce differently. Rising incomes can pay for investments in environmental improvement, and preventing the depletion or degradation of nature is much less expensive than trying to undo the damage.

86 Individuals and communities often lack information about environmental impacts or about low-cost ways to avoid damage. Governments and others must therefore actively promote environmental awareness. Awareness can be the most significant factor in motivating environmental action.

87 If sustainable development is to succeed, it must become the concern and commitment not just of Governments, but of all segments of society. Sustainable development means a commitment to using renewable resources and to avoiding the over-consumption of non-renewable resources. It means choosing products and production processes that have the least adverse impact on the environment. In agriculture, it means avoiding the excessive use of harmful, energy-intensive chemicals and preserving biodiversity. In all areas of public and private life it means a commitment to conserving natural resources and protecting the ecological equilibrium.

88 Setting priorities for international environmental policy is particularly complex. The costs of doing nothing may be borne by other nations, and the gains may not accrue to those that take the most difficult decisions.

89 Consideration must be given to problems at all levels. Some problems, such as damage to the ozone layer, are global. Transborder industrial pollution may be regional. Drinking-water contamination may be local in effect. The respective roles of regulation and incentives at different levels can be crucial. Norms and direct regulations will be necessary, but the use of taxes and licences can also achieve results.

90 The consequences of deforestation and environmental degradation have produced pressures that have touched off bitter conflicts. In a growing number of regions, poverty, resource degradation and conflict are becoming an all-too-familiar triangle. Throughout the world, refugees from the effects of environmental devastation and depletion place an added burden on already hard-pressed urban areas.

91 But while the spectre of resource-based conflict dramatizes the common stake that all nations have in addressing the challenge of environment and development, international cooperation is required in order effectively to address a wide range of common environment

and development interests. When the effects of environmental degradation cross national boundaries it is not possible to rely, as in an individual country, on a common legal framework, on uniform regulatory controls, on shared economic incentives or on the coercive powers of a national Government.

92   Solutions to international environmental problems must be based on common principles and rules of collaboration among sovereign States, backed up by persuasion and negotiation. Regional problems, with possible political implications, can arise when neighbouring countries share a common resource, such as international rivers or regional seas. There are also global environmental resources, such as the atmosphere and the oceans, that must be a target of multilateral action. In the case of resources that belong to one country but that are of value to the international community, ecological habitats and rare species, for example, individual States are entitled to international cooperation for the preservation of the common legacy.

93   Sustainability must be strengthened as a guiding principle of development. Partnership is required at all levels of the development effort; among different departments and levels of administration within States, as well as between international organizations, Governments and non-State actors. In short, true partnership is required between humanity and nature.

D. Justice as a pillar of society

94   Development does not take place in a vacuum, nor is it built upon an abstract foundation. Development takes place within a specific societal context and in response to specific societal conditions. It affects all aspects of society, and all aspects of society contribute to or detract from development. Economic growth and technological transformation affect human relationships, societal structures, values and lifestyles. Social and human resource development makes social and economic relations more harmonious, facilitates inclusiveness and societal cohesion, and provides a solid and adaptable foundation for achieving long-term progress.

95   Existing social conditions are the starting-point for development efforts. To a large extent, they determine its priorities and its direction. Throughout much of the developing world, poverty, disease and the need for education and sustainable livelihoods are the most urgent and compelling priorities for development. In many of the countries in transition, sudden economic hardship, decaying industries and infrastructures and profound social disorientation are problems that development must urgently address. Among the richest countries, the growth of a permanent and disaffected underclass, the arrival of increasing numbers of economic migrants and a rise in xenophobia and exclusionary attitudes are realities that must be faced as these societies continue to advance and develop.

96   People are a country's principal asset. Their well-being defines development. Their energy and initiative drive development. Their characteristics determine the nature and direction of sustainable human development. The benefits of investing in people, however, go beyond increasing the productivity of labour and facilitating access to global opportunities. A healthy, well-educated citizenry contributes to the social cohesion of a country and imparts a dynamism to all aspects of life and culture.

97   Absolute poverty, hunger, disease and illiteracy are the lot of one fifth of the world's population. There can be no more urgent task for development than to attack both the causes and the symptoms of these ills. It is a task that requires action and commitment. It is an agenda that requires the widest possible distribution of development efforts, the implementation of broad-based strategies and the orientation of development efforts towards projects that enhance people rather than national prestige.

98   Demographic growth rates affect the consumption and production patterns of societies. Beyond a certain point, however, unsustainable and unsupportable population growth can have adverse effects on development efforts globally. These effects in turn have profound implications for the use of natural resources such as water, wood, fuel and air. They affect the ability of Governments to supply the basic services that people require, including education and health care.

99 Fertility and mortality rates have societal implications that go beyond population counts. Reduction in fertility, for example, means smaller households and less time devoted to childbearing and rearing. These changes enable increased numbers of women to continue their formal education and to choose to work outside the home. Education further increases their chances of employment and enhances their ability to make choices in all aspects of life. Lower levels of mortality and fertility also result in the ageing of populations, a phenomenon that has significant implications for the labour force, dependency rates, social welfare services and health delivery systems.

100 Extended conflict has a dramatic impact on population profiles; the number of female-headed households increases as does the number of orphans and handicapped people. Close attention to these vulnerable populations is an immediate and major priority, for, without them, society itself cannot succeed. Once the family unit is reconstructed and the weak and most afflicted given care, they can provide the foundation for development efforts on a wider scale.

101 The importance of social integration as a development priority is evident worldwide, and among countries across the development spectrum. Manifestations of the lack of social integration are familiar: discrimination, fanaticism, intolerance, persecution. The consequences are also familiar: social disaffection, separatism, micronationalism and conflict.

102 The challenge of social integration is now increasingly internationalized. Large movements of people across international borders, seeking new and better lives, are critically affecting both national and international agendas. While millions of people flee from wars, famines and natural disasters, additional millions are migrating to find employment. The regulation of immigration has become a contentious political issue in many receiving countries, while political pressures to emigrate have added to social and economic tensions in many countries of departure. Emigrants can be among the most highly skilled and best educated, representing a serious loss of national resources and investment.

103 Until development on a global scale improves, large popula-

tions will continue to move across borders despite efforts to control or impede their flow. In some societies, resentment against migrants has fanned the flames of hatred and intolerance, and official policies have often seemed to condone separatism rather than promote social integration. Elsewhere, immigrant groups have resisted social integration. The treatment of migrants has become an issue of considerable tension in many bilateral relationships.

104 The enormous challenge of development cannot be undertaken by people whose every thought is bent towards getting enough to eat or recovery from debilitating sickness. A population that is illiterate and uneducated cannot hope to compete in a world economy that is becoming ever more complex and sophisticated. A society where women are discriminated against or lack equal opportunities cannot reach its full human potential.

105 While investment in physical capital is an important aspect of stimulating economic growth, investment in human development is an investment in long-term competitiveness and a necessary component of stable and sustainable progress. Investment in human resources must, therefore, be seen not merely as a by-product of economic growth, but rather as a powerful and necessary driving force for all aspects of development. A stable economy and a stable political order cannot be built in an unstable society. A strong social fabric is a prerequisite to sustainability.

106 The creation of an environment that will provide wide access to assets and opportunities may require governmental measures. Creating the political conditions which allow for adequate weight to be given to social development and the implementation of social development policies is also essential. These are major responsibilities of government, and of all the institutions of society. Governments should ensure that consideration is given to social and environmental factors in the framework of the market economy, and that emphasis is given to activities that promote human development throughout society. Education, health services, housing and social welfare are particular areas in which government action is often needed.

107 A vigorous civil society is indispensable to creating lasting and successful social development. Social development, if it is to take hold, must spring from society itself. Government must lead and facilitate, but government cannot, and should not, be the only force for social progress. Non-governmental organizations (NGOs), community organizations, private enterprise, worker's organizations and other groups must all be actively involved. Locally based NGOs, in particular, can serve as intermediaries and give people a voice and an opportunity to articulate their needs, preferences and vision of a better society. Policy makers should view such organizations not as rivals to government, but as partners. In countries where civil society is weak, strengthening civil society should be a major purpose of public policy.

108   In helping to create the conditions within which social development can take place, popular participation at all levels of society is of vital importance. In order to fulfil their potential, people must participate actively in formulating their own goals, and their voices must be heard in decision-making bodies as they seek to pursue their own most appropriate path to development.

109   Democracy and a vigorous civil society are particularly vital in helping to ensure that government is sensitive to the societal costs of its policies. In many countries, the necessary process of economic structural adjustment has had harsh social consequences. Rising consumer prices and declining employment and income have often been the most immediately visible effect of adjustment and transformation. The disproportionate impact of the resulting hardships on poor and vulnerable groups has been particularly devastating. A general decline in government expenditures in the social sector, as a result of heightened budgetary austerity, has compounded the suffering for many.

110   Structural adjustment remains a necessary prescription to remedy serious economic imbalance. But it should also be clear that human needs and priorities must not be neglected, and that adjustment and transformation must have a clear human focus. The laws of economics cannot be changed, but their social consequences can be eased. Flexibility is required. In the face of such challenges, Governments must be encouraged to stay the course, but greater care must also be taken to help Governments address the dire human consequences of such reforms.

111 The expansion of productive employment is central to the alleviation and reduction of poverty and the enhancement of social integration, yet increasing unemployment levels are prevalent worldwide. In many countries, higher levels of unemployment than in the past have been accompanied by significant declines in real wages among those who are employed. Among countries where full employment was previously the official norm, rapidly rising unemployment has had profound psychological consequences in addition to its severe economic and social impact. Among some countries, a prolonged period of economic retrenchment has produced the phenomenon of "jobless growth", and a more pervasive feeling of employment insecurity. Of the world labour force of 2.5 billion people, an estimated 30 per cent are not productively employed.

112 No single blueprint can be given for curing unemployment or expanding productive employment. Labour market measures, training and retraining programmes, targeted employment-creation schemes and macroeconomic policy can all affect employment levels. Since most jobs in the near future are likely to be created in the private sector, well-designed incentive structures have an important role to play in attracting and channelling private investment for employment growth. One of the tasks of the State is to create the enabling environment for the private sector to create more and better jobs. A fair and reliable legal framework, a stable investment environment and the maintenance of basic infrastructures are essential.

113 Because agriculture accounts for the bulk of the labour force in the developing world, measures aimed at boosting agricultural productivity and expanding and diversifying the range of farm and off-farm activities need to be regarded as a development priority. Food pricing policies, agricultural techniques, rural non-farm activities with employment linkages, rural infrastructure and environmentally appropriate conservation programmes are essential components of support for the rural sector. Agricultural research to increase yields should continue to be supported.

114 Employment potential is also affected by conditions in the international economy and the structure of the international economic environment. Trade barriers have a backward ripple effect, taking away productive jobs and livelihoods in producer countries and retarding the potential for economic growth.

115 Today, employment issues must be examined in an international context. In the countries in transition there has been a necessary move towards market-economy principles a process that has temporarily generated higher levels of unemployment than had previously been experienced. Among the richest industrialized countries, structural unemployment has increased. In addition, the growth of international competitiveness has led to many industries becoming obsolete and thousands of defence industry jobs disappearing. These shifts require the retraining of millions of workers. Among both types of economies, occupational mobility is an important part of employment creation. While economically efficient, occupational mobility can be a source of psychological and social disruption. Governments, enterprises and trade unions have an increased responsibility to facilitate worker adaptation and mobility and to offer training and social protection during transition periods.

116 A good general education at primary and secondary levels not only provides a broad knowledge base, but also lays a foundation for the subsequent acquisition of more narrowly defined skills, and for renewing, adapting or changing these skills to suit better the evolving needs of individuals and societies. Education facilitates equality of opportunity, thereby contributing to greater equity. Education that is both broad-based and flexible can be a driving force for progress in all dimensions of development: political, economic, environmental and social.

117 The significance of the social dimension to development must not only be recognized, but it must also be acted upon. The political profile of social development issues must be raised both nationally and internationally. Each country has a duty to address social development within its own society, and each also has a duty to contribute to progress towards a more global solution to these challenges. The present period provides an historic opportunity to do so in an environment that is relatively free from excessive ideological tensions. It is an opportunity to be seized and turned to advantage.

E. Democracy as good governance

118 The link between development and democracy is intuitive, yet it remains difficult to elucidate. While empirically, democracy and development appear in the long-term to be inseparable, events have not always pointed to a clear causal link between the two processes. In some countries, a certain level of development has been achieved and this has been followed at a later period by a trend towards democratization. In other countries, democratization has led the way to an economic revolution.

119 In viewing democracy in the context of development, processes and trends rather than events must be our focus. From this perspective, the natural connection between development and democracy becomes clearer. Just as development is a process rather than an event, so too must democracy be regarded as a process which grows and must be sustained over time. The World Conference on Human Rights stressed the mutually reinforcing interrelationship of democracy, development and respect for human rights.

120 Democracy and development are linked in fundamental ways. They are linked because democracy provides the only long-term basis for managing competing ethnic, religious, and cultural interests in a way that minimizes the risk of violent internal conflict. They are linked because democracy is inherently attached to the question of governance, which has an impact on all aspects of development efforts. They are linked because democracy is a fundamental human right, the advancement of which is itself an important measure of development. They are linked because people's participation in the decision-making processes which affect their lives is a basic tenet of development.

121 The accumulation of economic despair, and the lack of democratic means to effect change, have sparked or exacerbated violent and destructive impulses even within relatively homogeneous societies. Civil conflict and strife have increasingly become threats to international peace and profound obstacles to development. Ethnic antagonism, religious intolerance and cultural separatism threaten the cohesion of societies and the integrity of States in all parts of the world. Alienated and insecure minorities, and even majorities, have increasingly turned to armed conflict as a means of addressing social and political grievances.

122 Democracy is the only long-term means of both arbitrating and regulating the many political, social, economic and ethnic tensions that constantly threaten to tear apart societies and destroy States. In the absence of democracy as a forum for competition and a vehicle for change, development will remain fragile and be perpetually at risk.

123 Unrest and conflict can destroy in a few months progress towards development painstakingly achieved over the course of many years. In the eventual rush to settle old scores, redress perceived grievances and establish new Utopias, whatever gains that may have been achieved will be one of the many casualties.

124 Holding elections is only one element in democratization. Member States have sought and received United Nations assistance in facilitating decolonization, thereby implementing the right to self-determination, in designing procedures to smooth and facilitate transitions to democracy and in building democratic alternatives to conflict. United Nations support has also been provided for activities such as drafting constitutions, instituting administrative and financial reforms, strengthening domestic human rights laws, enhancing judicial structures, training human rights officials and helping armed opposition movements transform themselves into democratically competitive political parties.

125 Improving and enhancing governance is an essential condition for the success of any agenda or strategy for development. Governance may be the single most important development variable within the control of individual States.

126 In the context of development, improved governance has several meanings. In particular however, it means the design and pursuit of a comprehensive national strategy for development. It means ensuring the capacity, reliability and integrity of the core institutions of the modern State. It means improving the ability of government to carry out governmental policies and functions, including the management of implementation systems. It means accountability for actions and transparency in decision-making.

127 Regardless of ideology, geography or stage of development, societies lacking in democracy tend, over time, to resemble each other, with a relatively powerless middle class, a population constrained to silence and a ruling oligarchy which benefits itself through the management of a system of pervasive and often institutionalized corruption. People in a democracy have greater freedom to speak out against graft and corruption. Improved governance means that bureaucratic procedures help ensure fairness rather than enrich officials.

128 While democracy is not the only means by which improved governance can be achieved, it is the only reliable one. By providing for greater popular participation, democracy increases the likelihood that national development goals will reflect broad societal aspirations and priorities. By providing appropriate mechanisms and channels for governmental succession, democracy provides incentives to protect the capacity, reliability and integrity of core state institutions, including the civil service, the legal system and the democratic process itself. By establishing the political legitimacy of governments, democracy strengthens their capacity to carry out their policies and functions efficiently and effectively. By making Governments accountable to citizens, democracy makes particular Governments more responsive to popular concerns and provides added incentives for transparency in decision-making.

129 The mandate of the people to govern provides legitimacy; it does not carry with it, however, the guarantee of skill or wisdom. Democracy cannot instantly produce good governance, nor will democratic government immediately lead to substantial improvements in growth rates, social conditions or equality. By providing channels for participation of people in decisions which affect their lives, democracy brings government closer to the people. Through decentralization and strengthening of community structures, local factors relevant to development decisions can more adequately be taken into account.

130 Democracy leaves no room for complacency. Anti-democratic practices can be identified in those countries where democratic traditions have most deeply taken root. Chronically low voter turnouts, financing of candidates by special interests and the lack of transparency of certain institutions of government can be cited as specific examples. Similarly, the presence of a permanent underclass is a feature of many of the richest societies. Finally, the persistence of high levels of unemployment and the presence of foreign migrants have led to the revival of xenophobic, ultranationalist and fundamentally anti-democratic movements in some societies with the highest standards of living. These phenomena point towards a need to strengthen political development even in societies where democracy has long been considered secure.

131 Elsewhere, the release of pent-up frustrations resulting from decades of one-party rule has led to a confusion between multi-party elections and lasting democracy. While pluralism and parliaments are essential to the transition to democratic government, the demise of the one-party State does not ensure the ultimate triumph of democracy. The fragmentation of multi-ethnic societies and the difficult beginning of the transition to the market-economy have led to a revival of anti-democratic tendencies which seek to exercise political power.

132 The rise of anti-democratic forces, basing their appeal on popular disappointment with poor economic performance, is not confined to affluent societies or to societies in transition. Many societies throughout the developing world now face the difficult task of coping not only with the transition to democracy, but also with reform of their economies. Raised expectations and difficult economic conditions generated in the early stages of reform also pose a challenge to democratization. In many cases, involvement in civil or international conflicts further complicates the situation. Where resources are scarce and where the bulk of the population cannot satisfy its basic needs, political development is exceedingly difficult to achieve. Political progress is often obstructed by the struggle for economic and social advancement.

133 Sustaining democracy and development within States is closely linked to expanding democracy in relations among States and at all levels of the international system. Democracy in international relations provides the only basis for building mutual support and respect among nations. Without true democracy in international relations, peace will not endure, and a satisfactory pace of development cannot be assured.

134 Democracy within the family of nations is a principle that is integral to the system of international relations envisioned in the Charter of the United Nations. It is a principle that means affording to all States, large and small, the fullest opportunity to consult and to participate. It means the application of democratic principles within the United Nations itself. It means that all organs of the United Nations must be accorded, and play, their full and proper role. It will help maintain an equilibrium among the political, economic and social activities of the United Nations so that they may be mutually reinforcing.

135 Democracy in international relations also means respect for democratic principles in interactions taking place outside the United Nations. It means bilateral discussions instead of bilateral threats. It means respect for the integrity and the sovereignty of other nations. It means consultation and coordination in addressing problems of mutual concern. It means cooperation for development.

136 Dialogue, discussion and agreement are demanding activities. But they are the essence of democracy, within nations and within the family of nations. Above all, they are the principal means through which the society of States must strive to express its common will and achieve progress.

137 In this new era, when information, knowledge, communication and intellectual interchange are critical to economic and social success, democracy must be seen not only as an ideal, or an event, but also as a process which is essential to achieving tangible progress.

Democracy supplies the only long-term and sustainable route to successful development. Democratization within the international system permits voices for development not only to be heard but also to carry political weight. A more democratic world can facilitate cooperative work on an agenda for development.

138 The five dimensions of development outlined here, peace, the economy, the environment, society and democracy, are closely interlinked. These dimensions are not arbitrary, but emerge from a half-century of practical work by the United Nations and others with Governments, organizations and people. Achieving greater coherence, consensus and cooperation for development is considered in the following section.

III. The United Nations in development

A. Recognizing the actors

139 While the individual State is no longer the sole actor in development, each State continues to bear primary responsibility for its own development. Whether expressed as a responsibility of States or as a right of peoples, development requires competent governmental leadership, coherent national policies and strong popular commitment.

140 But few, if any, societies can pursue all aspects of development unaided. Development requires international cooperation and it requires that other actors assist States in their efforts. Bilateral assistance from one State to another amounts to some $62 billion annually. Such assistance is often given in the form of "tied-aid".

141 Each State has its own particular approach to development. Even within a single Government, related development issues are often dealt with by different departments. At present, a Government may be represented within an international development organization variously by its ministries of agriculture, environment, finance, economics and foreign affairs.

142 In terms of the range of ideas, funds, projects and groups engaged, development has emerged as a truly global endeavour. The actors in development, public and private, national and international, are growing in number and diversity. The sheer multiplicity of actors and agents now threatens to overwhelm development efforts in some societies. The overall endeavour calls for greater coherence. Moreover, the allocation of resources between various dimensions of development remains unbalanced, with the result that many activities, especially in the area of social development, remain underfinanced. Coordination and prioritization are, therefore, critical as each of the various entities involved has its particular objectives, agenda, constituency and mode of operation. There is a need to put in place a system of international cooperation that facilitates the mobilization of domestic resources and external assistance (both technical and financial) for peace, the economy, the environment, society and democracy.

143 The organs of the United Nations have been assigned by the Charter a set of roles in development which call for new levels of coordination. The General Assembly, through Chapters IV, IX and X of the Charter, is given fundamental responsibility for international economic and social cooperation. Throughout its first half-century, the Assembly has emerged as a universal forum for debate and action on development issues affecting all States. The Economic and Social Council, through functions and powers provided by Chapter X of the Charter, possesses a range of responsibilities for studying, initiating and coordinating issues relating to development. The Security Council, through the provisions of Chapter VII, can adversely affect the course of development within States to which sanctions apply, as well as in neighbouring and other States. The Secretariat is the source of substantive support, including technical advice and assistance on development needs in such fields as development planning and policies, statistics, energy, natural resources and public administration. (Annex I to the present report shows estimated expenditure of the United Nations and its funds and programmes.) With responsibilities scattered among various organs, the importance of coordination and coherence is clear. Through the regional commissions, the Secretariat promotes the coordination of intersectoral programmes and technical cooperation for the benefit of Member States.

144 The programmes and funds of the United Nations dispose of $3.6 billion annually for operational activities (see annex II). As their work goes forward, new trends are developing. A trend towards thematic and special purpose funding presents new challenges and opportunities for the United Nations Development Programme (UNDP) to support programmes through which recipient Governments can coherently address all dimensions of sustainable human development. Another trend is the shift in emphasis from development to relief activities. In the work of the World Food Programme (WFP), for example, while all-time record tonnages are being delivered, some three fifths by necessity are going for short-term emergency relief rather than for long-term development. Impelled by violence, social distress or economic need, nearly 20 million refugees and 25 million internally displaced persons, now require assistance. In 1993, some $1.115 billion was expended in this cause by the Office of the United Nations High Commissioner for Refugees (UNHCR).

145 The specialized agencies of the United Nations system have their own statutes, budgets and governing bodies. Together, they provide $6.3 billion in concessional flows and $7.8 billion in non-concessional-related lending as net disbursements. Specialized agencies derive about 40 per cent of their operational funds from United Nations programmes and funds. Member States also provide them with resources for specific projects. New trends are emerging. Over the years, the Bretton Woods institutions (the World Bank and the International Monetary Fund (IMF)) have been regarded as primarily focused on the immediate issues of macroeconomic stability and economic growth, leaving the long-term social aspects of development to other entities within the United Nations system. Changes in the course and character of global development are leading to a reassessment of this dichotomy. Firstly, the distinction between "hard" and "soft" issues has become blurred. Thus, the Bretton Woods institutions are now involved in social development and the design of social safety nets in conjunction with adjustment programmes. IMF is increasingly involved in providing advice and resources in the medium-term context to promote high-quality growth. The World Bank now considers environmental effects in making loans and sets aside funds to finance social dimensions of adjustment. Secondly, with the increasing magnitude of international lending and investment, World Bank lending decisions have become less decisive in their direct impact on development and more important as indicators of creditworthiness for private capital markets. Thirdly, conditionality has reduced the policy latitude of national Governments, thereby increasing the risks of domestic instability. Taken together, these trends indicate a need for greater interaction between the policy advice and country operations of the Bretton Woods institutions, and the approaches and practices of other actors in development.

146 Regional arrangements and organizations are a growing phenomenon in the world and provide development assistance of some $5.5 billion each year. Regionalism is neither incompatible with nor an alternative to internationalism as expressed through the United Nations. Regional cooperation is a necessity for development everywhere. Regional trade associations provide expanded markets for domestic enterprises, and encourage interregional agreements to facilitate trade. Regional assistance can address development across political boundaries and respond to practical needs wherever they arise. Water resources, electrification, transportation, communication and health systems can all benefit from region-wide approaches. Regional coordination can allocate transnational trade-offs and transcend lower level bureaucratic rivalries. But regionalization also carries with it the dangers of protectionism and bureaucratic layering. Careful management is required to ensure that regionalization facilitates the greater coordination that comprehensive development demands.

147 NGOs undertake projects valued at more than $7 billion annually. Long active in the search for peace, NGOs have often been at the scene of conflicts at an early stage, making a crucial contribution to the immediate relief of stricken populations and laying foundations for the reconstruction of war-torn societies. With flexible structures, the ability to mobilize private funds, and highly motivated staffs, NGOs possess a vast potential for the cause of development.

Over the past decade, the growth of NGOs in number and influence has been phenomenal. They are creating new global networks and proving to be a vital component of the great international conferences of this decade. The time has arrived to bring NGO and United Nations activities into an increasingly productive relationship of consultation and cooperation.

148 Private international investment flows have reached $1,000 billion per year, offering immense potential for job creation, technology transfer, training possibilities and trade promotion. The dynamism released by this process can revive stagnant economies and promote integration into the global economic system. Direct foreign investment can have a positive effect on the technological pool available to countries for development. Private enterprise is increasingly recognized as a positive factor in providing solutions to problems previously thought to be the special province of public authorities. In some countries private operators, for example, are providing effective public services such as telecommunications, transport, power, waste recycling and water supply. In many cases, subsidies to state companies could be replaced with targeted subsidies so that some users could be charged the true cost of the services and public money could be redirected to address broader needs.

149 Academic and scientific communities began centuries ago to weave a global fabric of productive scholarship and research. Today, thousands of such centres span the globe in a network of thought, experimentation, creativity and virtually instantaneous intellectual exchange. Their work increasingly ranges across disciplinary as well as political boundaries, rearranging and integrating old categories into new patterns of social utility. The scientific community forms a worldwide network, sharing certain fundamental interests, values and standards. It is a community that has an important part to play in addressing the great problems of development. Centres of science and technology are addressing questions of immediate practical importance to the everyday life of people, even as they bring the longer perspective of accumulated scientific and humanistic achievement to bear on current issues. Science can expand development options, through the development of new, safe, simple and effective methods of family planning, the development of environmentally benign energy sources, the improvement of agricultural techniques, better disease control, and in many other ways. Less recognized but of deep importance is research in the social sciences; the humanities and the arts. These not only enrich human existence, as has long been recognized, but also are casting new light on many of the essential characteristics and needs of life in the human community in all its many forms.

150 Grass-roots organizations, such as religious communities, neighbourhood associations and self-help groups, understand the interrelatedness of economic, social, human and sustainable development. As they address the needs of small communities otherwise often overlooked, the learning process in development flows not only to but from their direction. Grass-roots and community associations suffer from a low level of funding and are often in need of technical assistance. Although funds should primarily be raised locally, the United Nations is able to support activities at the micro-level by assisting grass-roots organizations.

151 The sheer number of actors in development today, the global trends that their activities reflect and the interrelationship of problems and the mechanisms for their solution all highlight the urgent need for greater awareness and more determined commitment.

B. Information, awareness and consensus

152 Addressing the global development challenge requires building a common awareness of the many dimensions of development, and a better appreciation of the importance of the various actors in development. Raising levels of awareness and creating a global consensus, help to create what can best be called a "culture of development". Defining a culture of development implies more than universal access to shared information networks. A culture of development, as has been noted, implies that all actions are considered in their relation to development. Based on this universal culture of development, which is rapidly evolving in the closing years of the twentieth century, the United Nations becomes an increasingly effective forum for establishing universal standards of conduct.

153 The United Nations, universal in its membership and comprehensive in its mandate, has the responsibility and the ability to draw global attention to issues of broad importance. The United Nations can help alert, inform and maintain international attention on problems not susceptible to quick or easy solutions. In the last few years, the United Nations has been indispensable in drawing attention to the need for environmental action, in addressing the impact of demographic change, in the cause of human rights and in bringing an international focus on development in all its aspects.

154 A sound informational foundation is vital in formulating all aspects of economic policy. Governmental and private-sector planning and decision-making can only be effective if the information relied upon is accurate and up to date. The public's participation in economic, social and political activities cannot be meaningful unless it is also well-informed.

155 Without an adequate informational base, countries operate at a disadvantage in bilateral and multilateral negotiations. National access to information on international economic, demographic, social and environmental conditions is essential not only to informed decision-making, but also to competitive and effective participation in international markets.

156 As an active collector of data and statistics, the United Nations system is an important yet sometimes under-utilized informational asset for Member States. The United Nations system has been at the forefront of efforts to provide technical cooperation on establishing and upgrading information and communications infrastructures. These efforts are widely valued, but require the increasingly active support of Member States.

157 The Organization shapes common and comparable approaches to organizing and structuring data, promotes unified standards for technical communication, improves data collection methods, facilitates the mutually beneficial exchanges of international data and information, helps analyse and evaluate data and provides training and assistance in the use of information.

158 The United Nations system has been a pioneer in mounting international cooperation for the collection, analysis and use of data for population planning, health care, governance and public administration, job creation, wage and income questions and social welfare needs; all designed to enable peoples and Governments to make more informed decisions. The United Nations is seeking to quantify human progress in a new way, providing a statistical picture of human development that goes beyond measuring per capita gross national product. The UNDP *Human Development Report* has initiated a rethinking of the parameters by which development is measured.

159 Reliable statistics monitoring a nation's economic activity and tracking economic, social and environmental change are essential to informed decision-making and a necessary foundation for successful national development. A new System of National Accounts, providing a framework within which countries can gain a fresh perception of their economic statistics, and enhancing their use of such data, was pioneered by the United Nations in cooperation with IMF, the World Bank, the Organization for Economic Cooperation and Development and the Commission of the European Union.

160 New ways of collecting and disseminating environmental statistics and indicators are being tested in a number of countries through a variety of United Nations technical cooperation programmes. This undertaking is particularly important as the gap in availability, quality, coherence and accessibility of data among countries has been increasing. Information deficits continue to impair the capacity of many economies to make informed decisions concerning the environment and development.

161 Collection and analysis of information is a prerequisite not only for informed discussion, but also for formulating acceptable and workable solutions. Reliable, standardized information provides the common language in which all can participate in the culture of development. If information is not reliable, available and presented in a usable form, consensus will be elusive and successful action highly unlikely.

162 In recent years, global international conferences have provided Member States and others with opportunities to think together about the major choices facing the world in the process of development, thus promoting a consensual culture of development. Such global gatherings focus on strategic issues at the highest level, enabling Member States to bring their national policies into line with values and principles endorsed by the international community as a whole. They give political direction and a new momentum to international efforts, while providing inspiration and encouragement to States, to organizations and to people.

163 UNCED brought an unprecedented commitment by world leaders to a shared set of objectives for the future: Agenda 21,[1/] the first international agreement expressing a global consensus and a political commitment at the highest levels to action on environment and economic progress, encompassed in a programme of sustainable development. Since UNCED, environmental concerns have been firmly placed in the mainstream of the culture of development. The Global Conference on the Sustainable Development of Small Island Developing States, held in Barbados from 25 April to 6 May 1994, further defined the responsibilities of small island States, and of the international community, in the pursuit of sustainable development.

164 The World Conference on Human Rights was held at Vienna from 14 to 25 June 1993. In the Vienna Declaration and Programme of Action,[2/] the Conference reaffirmed "the right to development, as established in the Declaration on the Right to Development, as a universal and inalienable right and an integral part of fundamental human rights". From the proclamation of the Universal Declaration of Human Rights in 1948 to its decision to create a United Nations High Commissioner for Human Rights, the General Assembly has underscored its expectation of conformity with agreed international principles of human rights.

165 In September 1994, the International Conference on Population and Development, to be held at Cairo, will address the impact of demographic factors on development and take up the challenge of creating a truly people-centred development.

166 The World Summit for Social Development, to be held in

1995, the Fiftieth Anniversary of the United Nations, could be a synthesizing event of world significance. It is increasingly evident that a just society cannot accept high levels of unemployment. A stable society cannot permit entire groups to be excluded from the fruits of development. A secure society cannot exist without social safety nets for its most disadvantaged members. A determined global effort is needed to raise awareness and political commitment to effective action, both national and international. The World Summit will provide an indispensable opportunity to draw past achievements together as a coherent whole and to set forth the new areas for concerted effort. It should elevate the social development agenda to an equal level with economic growth by strengthening the national and international institutional structures dealing with social issues, facilitating coordination of their operations with those in economic areas, and providing adequate supportive finance and other assistance.

167 The process will continue in 1995 at Beijing with the fourth in the series of world conferences on women. The United Nations, largely through the efforts of the Commission on the Status of Women, which was established in 1946, has helped to develop the legal basis for the promotion of equal rights for women and has been in the forefront of policy development, political commitment and institutional development. A further milestone was the adoption, in 1979, of the Convention on the Elimination of All Forms of Discrimination against Women. The Convention now has 132 States Parties who report regularly on the implementation of its provisions. The Convention on the Rights of the Child and the Vienna Declaration of the World Conference on Human Rights have also spelled out institutional standards for women's rights. The vision for the next century should build on these achievements and fully reflect a gender perspective.

168 In 1996, the Habitat II conference on human settlements, the "City Summit" will discuss a programme of action designed to make urban areas, where the majority of the world's population will live, safe, humane, healthy and affordable.

169 In addition to Member States, international efforts to strengthen the global culture of development must also encompass the broader international community. The contribution of non-State actors to the culture of development was clearly demonstrated during UNCED and the World Conference on Human Rights. NGOs and concerned individuals claimed their rightful share in creating a culture of development.

170 Within countries, elements of the civil society, including political parties, trade unions, parliamentarians and NGOs, have become increasingly important in creating and obtaining public support for development efforts on the one hand, and tangible development assistance on the other. Non-official groupings and movements now make up networks that help shape the direction of development policy and deliver practical results. To be successful, political consensus-building must embrace all.

171 By taking the initiative, highlighting issues of special concern and advancing realistic solutions, actors at all levels can help to shape the outcome of international efforts on the full range of global human concerns. Little of lasting value is possible until people and Governments share a political vision for progress, and have the political will to achieve it.

C. Norms, standards and treaties

172 Positive international action can only be achieved through cooperation. International law provides both the vehicle and the framework for turning ideas and intentions into action. In codifying the rights, duties, obligations and principles of international actors, international law not only provides the actual foundation upon which cooperation is built, but it likewise defines the terms of that cooperation, and also its limitations.

173 Forging multilateral agreement is the essence of international law, whether embodied in the form of non-binding norms, internationally recognized standards or binding obligations. By raising the political profile and public visibility of issues, multilateral agreements can galvanize interest and become a focal point for action. By creating a common framework for addressing problems, multilateral agreements can enhance coordination and promote coherence. By establishing common parameters and basic rules, multilateral agreements can facilitate international interaction and exchange. By establishing a common legal and political framework for action, multilateral agreements can provide a firm basis from which to assess and monitor international efforts. As practical mechanisms for forging consensus and pursuing solutions, multilateral agreements are the key to achieving meaningful international action in support of development.

174 The General Assembly has made numerous important contributions towards the establishment of an international framework for development cooperation. Assembly resolution 47/181 on an Agenda for Development refers in this context to the Declaration on International Economic Cooperation, in particular the Revitalization of Economic Growth and Development of the Developing Countries, the International Development Strategy for the Fourth United Nations Development Decade, the Cartagena Commitment, the United Nations New Agenda for the Development of Africa in the 1990s, the Programme of Action for the Least Developed Countries for the 1990s, and the various consensus agreements and conventions, especially Agenda 21, adopted at UNCED.

175 Galvanizing interest and becoming a focal point for action is both the aim and the impact of many multilateral agreements. The process of consensus-building and codification raises the political profile of important issues as States and constituencies seek to advance or defend their particular interests, perspectives and agendas through the proposed agreement. International debate and discussion frequently boost the public visibility of the issues at stake, often generating new public awareness, interest and involvement.

176 The treaties, conventions and standards adopted in connection with UNCED exemplify the broad impact that the process of international consensus-building and codification can have. Years of study and preparation, the catalytic effect of a world gathering at the highest level and the drive to codify specific actions and commitments, brought universal attention to the urgent need to halt further deterioration of our environment, and to the overriding importance of pursuing development that is environmentally sound and sustainable. By putting environmental concerns on the agenda of States worldwide, and by doing so in a manner that compelled States to contemplate provisions and proposals, the process produced useful and much needed action, expanded public awareness of environmental issues worldwide and led throughout the world to valuable public policy appraisals on many of the topics of most concern.

177 In addition to galvanizing interest and opinion, multilateral agreements can also serve as a focal point for action. The United Nations Convention on the Law of the Sea,[3/] for example, now provides a mechanism for addressing development questions related to all aspects of the use of the sea and its resources. As new technologies and the hunger for new resources increase the capacity of nations to exploit the ocean's resources, the Convention provides a universal legal framework for rationally managing marine resources and an agreed set of principles to guide consideration of the numerous issues and challenges that will continue to arise. From navigation and overflights to resource exploration and exploitation, conservation and pollution and fishing and shipping, the Convention provides a focal point for international deliberation and for action.

178 In the context of international cooperation within the framework of multilateral conventions and understandings, international humanitarian efforts have included action such as the establishment of "emergency relief corridors", the growing use of United Nations peace-keepers for humanitarian missions, preventing the slaughter of innocent civilians, investigating alleged violations of international law and facilitating national reconciliation. By working through the operation of international humanitarian norms, conventions and standards to strengthen the practical foundations of international cooperation, the international community has revealed the great potential of multilateral arrangements to serve both as a catalyst for action and as mechanism for achieving results.

179 Also integral to the role of international law in contributing to development is its capacity to enhance coordination in the execution of policies and promote coherence in their formulation and design. Directly and indirectly, multilateral norms, standards and treaties help to advance these objectives in concrete and meaningful ways.

180 Where individual action is insufficient to achieve satisfactory results, or where cooperation with others could markedly improve the effectiveness of such actions, coordination is clearly desirable. In regulating international air transportation, for example, individual action would be ineffective. Preventing further deterioration of the ozone layer, similarly, can only be achieved if individual efforts and actions are coordinated. Multilateral agreements designed to address these issues necessarily serve as essential mechanisms for achieving coordination.

181 Promoting coherence and compatibility in international policy-making is a closely related objective, and one that is equally essential. To the extent that multilateral agreements foreclose certain policy options and promote others, narrowing through compromise and consensus-building the scope for disparate policy strategies, such agreements promote coherence and compatibility in international policy-making. Rewarding certain practices and punishing others, prohibiting certain actions and encouraging others, enshrining certain principles and rejecting others, these are the mechanisms through which norms, standards and treaties operate and through which greater policy coherence and compatibility is established.

182 By promoting biodiversity, for example, multilateral environmental agreements necessarily advance some national development options and policies while limiting or eliminating others. By establishing particular pollution emission standards, multilateral agreements necessarily advance a class of policies designed to restrict certain types or levels of activity, and preclude development or industrial strategies that would be incompatible with such standards. The result in both cases is greater international coherence and consistency in policy-making.

183 In a world where people increasingly interact beyond the confines of national boundaries, it is especially desirable that there be processes and a set of rules for governing private legal relationships of an international nature. Establishing common procedures and agreeing on rules for resolving conflicts of law is not only useful in facilitating commerce, but it also contributes greatly to the building of peaceful and stable international relations. Together, these efforts at cooperation facilitate interaction and development and help to bring practical coherence to the multiplicity of regulations generated by national systems of law.

184 Specific international conventions now operate with respect to an increasingly wide range of private international interactions. In the legal sphere, international conventions now cover issues such as the service of process, evidence taking, the enforcement of judgements and international conflicts of law. In the field of family law, important international agreements have been negotiated. In the commercial sphere, international conventions facilitate and expedite a wide range of activities from financial transactions to international rules for the sale of goods.

185 The vital importance of common action is particularly evident in international efforts to establish broad rules and principles to govern interactions between nations. Multilateral agreements provide for overseeing implementation of international labour standards, governing the management of air routes, regulating the use of international telecommunications frequencies, facilitating the international exchange of mail, monitoring world weather patterns and promoting international interaction in a wide range of other important areas.

186 Multilateral agreements also embody and reflect existing efforts to fashion globally acceptable rules of trade. The United Nations, through the United Nations Conference on Trade and Development (UNCTAD), has helped developing countries to obtain preferential treatment for their exports through the establishment of the Generalized System of Preferences, and has promoted the adoption of international commodity agreements and agreed principles for the control of restrictive business practices. The General Agreement on Tariffs and Trade (GATT) and the recently completed Uruguay Round of multilateral trade negotiations, illustrate the impact that multilateral cooperation can have in facilitating commerce and promoting development. It is estimated that global trade will increase by as much as $50 billion as a result of the agreement reached during the Uruguay Round. Throughout the international community, the positive impact of this stimulus to employment, production and trade will be significant.

187 The Uruguay Round is a vivid example of the positive impact that multilateral agreements can have on development, through facilitating, expediting and encouraging international trade and commerce. Among the many other significant examples are the United Nations Convention on Transit Trade of Land-locked States, the United Nations Convention on the Carriage of Goods by Sea, and the United Nations Convention on Contracts for the International Sale of Goods.

188 Providing a basis from which to assess and monitor international efforts, whether in support of development or in other fields, is also an essential part of the importance of pursuing multilateral agreements. As a result of international agreements, the International Labour Organization (ILO) is able to monitor labour practices worldwide. The United Nations Framework Convention on Climate Change[4/] provides for international review of national policies affecting climate change and for international monitoring of greenhouse emissions. In these instances, and in many others, multilateral agreements lay the foundation and provide the basis for information gathering, for compliance monitoring and for enforcement processes.

189 In the field of human rights, in particular, the importance of multilateral agreements in establishing both a basis and a right for monitoring and assessing the conduct of States is particularly evident. Not only do such agreements provide a standard against which conduct can be measured, but they also provide an agreed international basis for involvement in monitoring compliance. Multilateral agreements thus enable the international community to act upon the principle that humanity dignity is a concern that transcends national boundaries and national distinctions.

190 Indeed, the notion that individual human rights can be protected by the international community is one of the great practical and intellectual achievements of international law. Through the mechanisms and procedures of international law, international norms, standards, covenants and treaties now provide a standard of accountability and a legal basis for international action in support of human rights and humanitarian causes.

191 Agreeing on practical measures to implement a common approach to problems is the essence of what the multilateral agreements seek to achieve. By providing a framework for international cooperation, international law makes an important and very tangible contribution to virtually all aspects of global development. Through the coordination of disparate policies and efforts, the promotion of goals and targets, the establishment of norms and standards and the negotiation of treaties and conventions, international law provides both a vehicle for cooperation and a mechanism for action.

192 As the leading proponent of international law, and as the most important forum of international cooperation, the United Nations has a central role to play in enhancing the scope and effectiveness of multilateral cooperation, particularly as that cooperation is projected into international norms, standards and precepts. In this role, the United Nations has a special responsibility to promote and support the effective participation of all countries concerned in the negotiation, implementation, review and governance of international agreements or instruments.

D. Operations, commitment and change

193 The United Nations provides a forum for political consensus-building, a vehicle for international cooperation and a source of policy analysis and information. But for millions of people throughout the world, the United Nations is also an important operational organization, working to achieve practical outcomes.

194 In the developing world, and in countries in transition or in distress, the United Nations works to bring the benefits of development directly to people. These activities in the field take many forms. Working through its programmes and funds, as well as the Secretariat, the Organization helps to design development initiatives, supports development schemes and projects, provides technical training and capacity-building and assists Governments in the formulation of their overall development strategies.

195 Because Member States have primary responsibility for their own development, United Nations development activities are carried out in close collaboration with Governments and local communities. Local infrastructures are an important part of those efforts. Many activities are also conducted through NGOs and other non-State institutions. Other efforts are carried out by the Organization directly.

196 Through its efforts in the field, the United Nations plays a much needed and often unique role. In particular, the Organization's field activities help to translate international decisions into local action and strategies, to support useful non-commercial development initiatives, to advance development efforts in sensitive sectors and to pioneer new areas and new types of development assistance.

197 The enormous challenges that confront humanity require international cooperation. But agreement is only the starting-point for action. The United Nations field programmes provide a vital bridge between the formulation of broad international agreements and the ability of countries to translate those agreements into national action. Its global experience and perspective make the Organization a vital source of practical support, as Member States address the broad common issues that confront modern society. Without such assistance, many Member States would lack the familiarity with issues or the immediate capacity for action that can be required for progress. In the aftermath of UNCED, the United Nations, when asked, has helped Member States to identify necessary action, draft rules and policies and establish mechanisms to monitor and enforce environmental objectives.

198 In many sectors that are vital to development prospects, only the United Nations can demonstrate both the impartiality and the expertise necessary to achieve results. Development policies affecting public administration, governance and democratization are critical examples. Governments and societies that recognize the need for change may hesitate to contemplate outside assistance, for fear that that assistance may eventually open the way to outside pressure or control. In many vital sectors of development, the United Nations can draw on a long record of sensitivity and the impartiality and experience to both serve and assist national development efforts. It is a service for which many Member States will continue to rely upon the United Nations, and one that the Organization must continue to be able to provide.

199 United Nations field activities have also played a valuable role in pioneering new types and areas of development assistance. From a post-war emphasis on the provision of long-term foreign experts and consultants, resources are increasingly being directed to strengthening national capacity and expertise. Having demonstrated the need for many of its earlier areas of focus, and generated new sources of support, the United Nations must continuously evaluate whether particular areas of endeavour continue to warrant its full-scale involvement.

200 For the Organization itself, and for the international community as a whole, the field activities of the United Nations and the Organization's active development presence worldwide also have a broader significance. The United Nations standing and moral authority in international affairs generally, and its ability as an institution to grasp and apply itself to the human challenges of development, are closely linked to the Organization's presence and efforts in the field.

201 Through its fundamental commitment to working for human betterment, the United Nations most firmly and securely establishes its credentials and its credibility as an instrument for world peace. Worldwide, the United Nations flag stands as a symbol of its commitment not only to peace, but also to progress. The Organization's overall efforts are immeasurably strengthened by the visibility of its commitment to and activities on behalf of development. This moral commitment continues to define the work of the United Nations in the eyes of those who most look to and depend upon the Organization for support. This moral authority cannot be built upon abstractions, but only upon real service to people.

202 Throughout the Organization, and in all of its activities, the experience of staff who are working in the field to advance development adds an invaluable source of balance, perspective and understanding. The present agenda itself owes much to that broad store of practical human experience.

203 Through its field offices, theories are tested by concrete experience. Problems are considered in a more practical context. Through its presence in the field, the Organization not only learns about people but also learns directly from the people it serves.

204 It is clear, however, that the United Nations operations for development cannot engage or hope to solve every problem of development around the world. Practical activities must be designed to achieve cumulative results and to affect those particular problems for which even partial solutions will enhance the prospects for durable progress. In short, the underlying concept of operations for development is to go beyond the relief of distress to create enduring foundations for progress.

205 Assessing the precise impact of particular strategies is rarely possible in the short term. For the United Nations, however, development is a long-term commitment. The impact of efforts on the ground has helped to achieve significant progress. Emphasis on health services in the field helped, for example, to ensure the eradication of smallpox, the widespread immunization of children, and a dramatic cut in child death rates worldwide. Recognition of the importance of a common cultural heritage helped inspire efforts to preserve sites such as Abu Simbel, the Acropolis and Angkor Wat. Revelation of the deteriorating condition of the planet has resulted in changed thinking and in concrete efforts worldwide to reverse or repair the damage.

206 National capacity-building has been a key component of progress. In many cases, United Nations development efforts in the field have markedly increased the capacity of States to initiate and to sustain their development efforts. Equally vital, the Organization's presence has sometimes prevented the unravelling of development efforts, bridging critical gaps and compensating for deteriorating infrastructures.

207 While hard to measure, a half-century of technical cooperation and training has left an important legacy of increasing local expertise. This contribution is of vital importance. Unless people have the capacity to carry forward their own development, progress will remain uneven, and development will not be secure.

208 By establishing an environment, a framework and often an umbrella for development activities, the United Nations not only contributes directly to development, but it also facilitates the development activities of many other actors. The presence established by the Organization can help to create a climate more receptive to development cooperation, and more encouraging for other actors. In times of tension and instability, in particular, the international presence that the United Nations symbolizes can be vital in maintaining the momentum and the capacity to pursue development.

209 More generally, the priorities identified by the United Nations have often provided a basis for other actors to become involved and to participate. Agreements negotiated by the Organization have often provided a context within which other actors could also be involved. For the Organization itself, and for the international community in general, the United Nations presence in the field is a vital asset in the service of development.

E. Priority setting and coordination

210 The concept of development, as it emerges from the present report, involves several interrelated dimensions and a multiplicity of actors. The setting of priorities and coordination are imperative.

211 Each dimension of development is vital to the success of all others, as well as to the core concept of human-centred progress. Successful development cannot be achieved by pursuing any one dimension in isolation, nor can any one dimension be excluded from the development process. Without peace, human energies cannot be productively employed over time. Without economic growth, there will be a lack of resources to apply to any problem. Without a healthy environment, productivity will devour the basis of human progress. Without societal justice, inequalities will consume the best efforts at positive change. Without political participation in freedom, people will have no voice in shaping their individual and common destiny.

212 Limited resources and domestic and foreign constraints mean that choices must be made and priorities must be set. There are times when efforts to achieve some aspects of development are postponed. In some countries, for example, the short-term effects of economic reform may threaten political stability.

213 The coordination of activities and assistance is essential to achieve the maximum impact from development resources, and the true benefits of prioritizing efforts. Coordination means a clear allocation of responsibilities, an effective division of labour among the many actors involved in development, and a commitment by each of those actors to work towards common and compatible goals and objectives. Individual development actors must strive to make their efforts complementary and contributory, rather than isolated or competing. Coordination, so viewed, must guide the actions of each of these actors and the interactions among them.

214 The agenda on which all national, regional and global participants must cooperate includes international peace and security, economic progress, the environment, social justice, democracy and good governance. All must be part of a single endeavour. In the past, the international community has achieved success through prioritizing its resources and coordinating its efforts; in eradicating disease, in fighting famine, in working to protect the environment and in seeking to limit the proliferation of weapons of mass destruction. The prioritization of development efforts and the coordination of development actors are required at all levels of activity. Worldwide issues, such as the struggle against the human immunodeficiency virus (HIV) and acquired immunodeficiency syndrome (AIDS) require coordination among States, international and regional organizations, NGOs and agencies. In other cases, coordination must focus on a specific region or segment of society. Donors need to coordinate among themselves; recipients need to coordinate within their national systems.

215 Because development must be understood as a multifaceted, open-ended undertaking, and because development efforts must respond to particular national needs, priorities and circumstances, no single theory or set of priorities can be applied to the development efforts of all countries at any one time. But because development requires a perpetual balancing of priorities and emphasis and the continual reassessment of needs and policies, the role and importance of good government in promoting development cannot be overestimated. Because development must be an international endeavour, governance is an issue whose importance and impact may extend beyond particular national borders.

216 Governments must decide when to support difficult policies, and when to resist powerful pressures, both foreign and domestic. Good government implies the wisdom and the historical responsibility to know when to let market forces act, when to let civil society take the lead, and when government should intervene directly.

217 National development strategies must strive to ensure that development programmes and projects are consistent and coherent. In view of the large number of actors and agendas involved, within countries as well as internationally, fragmentation and inconsistency are frequent problems. Domestically, the challenge is to frame a coherent and comprehensive vision of development. Internationally, the challenge is to marshal efforts and resources most effectively in support of national development objectives.

218 As each society considers its development choices, the international community must act wisely. Persuasion, not pressure, is likely to produce the most determined effort and the most lasting results. As national Governments are primarily responsible for development, the recognition of the complexity of their task is the first responsibility of supportive international development actors.

219 Successful coordination can only be achieved if there is a will to work together. Mechanisms and structures can be developed to address areas of duplication, overlap and inconsistency. But better mechanisms and structures cannot compel or ensure cooperation, nor can they substitute for political will. Unless donors are prepared to cooperate rather than compete, unless agencies are willing to work as partners rather than rivals and unless organizations have the courage to measure the success of their efforts by the progress that they achieve, duplication, overlap and inconsistency will continue to hamper development efforts.

220 Development priorities or models cannot be imposed by the international community upon particular peoples. This is one of the lessons we must take from past efforts. But the international community can and must determine how best to maximize international development resources and achieve greater consistency and coordination among international development actors.

221 The country strategy note offers an important new vehicle for strengthened coordination. Through this approach, countries can work with the United Nations to design development projects and prioritize the use of development funds. The wide application of this technique to development assistance could have a significant impact. At present, and in the absence of a fully comprehensive approach covering all external aspects of development cooperation, the prioritization and coordination of international development efforts, both intergovernmental and non-governmental, remains an urgent need.

222 The resident coordinator system provides a valuable mechanism for better integrating development assistance into the overall country programme framework. Tapping into the capacity of the United Nations system as a whole, the resident coordinator aims to ensure that the extensive operational capacities of the Organization are totally supportive of national objectives and fully utilized to build national capacity. The resident coordinator can help to ensure that economic and social research and policy analysis, operational activities, humanitarian assistance and the promotion of human rights, support and reinforce each other at the national level. The resident coordinator system must continue to be strengthened.

223 The United Nations, as an organization that is both universal in its membership and comprehensive in its mandate, has an especially important role to play both in facilitating the establishment of international development priorities and in promoting coordination and cooperation among the many development actors. In raising awareness, supplying information and providing a forum for consensus building, in working to further cooperation through the establishment of norms, standards and treaties, and, especially, as an actor on the ground and in the field, the United Nations contributes to development efforts.

224 While prioritization and coordination are necessary considerations for all organizations and institutions, these requirements are especially vital to the effective working of an organization that is as diverse in its composition and as broad in its mandate as is the United Nations.

225 The Charter of the United Nations itself recognizes the special importance of coordination within the United Nations system, assigning to the Economic and Social Council, operating under the authority of the General Assembly, the important and difficult task of coordinating the policies and activities of the United Nations and its numerous specialized agencies. The Council provides a ready and potentially powerful vehicle for helping to prioritize the allocation of international resources for development. Coordination must not only encompass Governments and intergovernmental institutions, but it must also take into account the actions of the many important non-governmental actors in development.

226 A number of United Nations bodies already benefit from the participation of representatives of business, labour and consumer and other communities. New ways are needed to involve such actors in deliberations at all levels of the development effort.

227 Over the years, the absence of clear policy guidance from the General Assembly, and the lack of effective policy coordination and control by the Economic and Social Council has resulted in an overall lack of cohesion and focus within the system. At all levels, among the central organs, the programmes and the regional commissions, there has been a steady proliferation of subsidiary bodies and an increasing lack of policy coherence. The revitalized Council could make a significant contribution to establishing greater policy coherence and coordination within the United Nations system as a whole.

228 The United Nations system constitutes an unparalleled body of knowledge and expertise at the disposal of developing countries. Bringing the strength of the system together at country level requires a new commitment to coordination, impelled by unity of purpose. Through UNDP, its central funding mechanism, the United Nations has a unique global network of country offices which provide an infrastructure for the Organization's operational activities worldwide and enable it to respond flexibly and rapidly to changing national priorities.

229 The Bretton Woods institutions, as specialized agencies, are an integral part of the United Nations system. They are important sources of development finance and policy advice. They are increasingly active in technical assistance, which has the potential of creating overlap with the central funding role of UNDP, and in areas where competence exists in other specialized agencies. Special attention needs to be given to considering how these institutions and other organizations of the system could collaborate more closely on the basis of their respective areas of comparative strength. More systematic use of capital assistance from the Bretton Woods institutions in a coordinated, complementary and mutually reinforcing manner with technical assistance funding provided through UNDP and the specialized agencies is warranted in operational activities.

230 The capacity of the United Nations to reflect in its own policies and activities the interrelationships outlined in the present report will, to a large extent, depend upon the effectiveness of its coordination mechanisms and structures. But the United Nations cannot make decisions for its Member States. The present agenda's purpose is to offer guidelines for thought and action by each Member State.

IV. Conclusion: the promise of development

231 A culture of development, in which every major dimension of life is considered as an aspect of development, is emerging as a result of immense and agonizing effort. The possibilities for common understanding and cooperative, coordinated action are available as never before.

232 In the past few years near-universal recognition has been achieved of the need for fresh consideration of ways in which the goals of peace, freedom, justice and progress may be pursued in a dramatically transformed global context. A culture of development can encompass these goals in a single, comprehensive vision and framework for action. At the basis of this culture, there is the fundamental commitment of the Charter to "the dignity and worth of the human person". The institution of the United Nations is irreplaceable.

233 Development has to be oriented towards each person in the world. Beyond this must arise a recognition that this human community includes the generations yet to come. The record of this century has demonstrated the disastrous consequences when the living are asked to suffer on behalf of a utopian future, or when the present generation is heedless of the welfare of those yet to be born. If one extreme characterized earlier decades of this century, the other has more recently obstructed our vision.

234 Signs of a global era of development can be observed. They offer a paradox. The agricultural and industrial revolutions are now being succeeded by an age of information, communication and advanced technology. This presents the potential for freeing humanity from limits of time, place and resources that in the past were regarded as given. At the same time, however, these changes are accompanied by old forces that test the human condition in new ways; natural and human disasters, demography, disease, political confrontation, cultural and religious animosity, unemployment and ecological decay. These scourges are as old as humanity itself, but they have taken on freshly virulent forms and combinations.

235 From an understanding of development as limited to transferring funds and expertise from the haves to the have-nots, the perspective has shifted towards a broader concept encompassing the full range of human endeavour. The welfare of future generations must not be compromised by incurring debts that cannot be repaid, whether financial, social, demographic or environmental. Equally important is the recognition of the responsibility of the earth's present inhabitants to make the best use of the hard-won ideas, ideals and institutions handed down to us by our predecessors. Progress is not inherent in the human condition; retrogression is not inconceivable.

236 If the human community is to continue to advance, it is necessary to build respectfully upon what we have been given, to recognize that current achievements must be accessible to all, and to ensure that the work we leave behind stands not as a structure in need of repair but as a platform for future progress. This must be more than a matter for rhetoric. With this in mind, annexed to the present report is an inventory of United Nations work for development (see annexes I and II).

237 Whether this vision is fulfilled or not will be measured by what this living generation of the world's peoples and their leaders make or fail to make of the United Nations. Created at a unique moment of unanimity, dedicated to purposes even more expansive than its founders understood, embodying the best and most comprehensive purpose of the world's peoples, and provided with the mechanisms required to bring practical results, the Organization stands at the meeting point of past, present and future.

238 The intricate nature of the present world crisis must be grasped in its entirety before effective action to resolve it will be possible. The concepts of collective security, fundamental human rights, international law and social progress for all are being corroded by ethnocentrism, isolationism, cultural animosity and economic and social debilitation. Even the concept of the State as the foundation-stone of international cooperation is being damaged by those who define it in exclusionary terms and others who question its contemporary relevance and efficacy.

239 These concerns are felt in a context of unprecedented global change. Ecological, technological, demographical and social movements seem beyond the capacity of traditional forms of international management. Faced with such a challenge, some even suggest that the modern project of international cooperation be abandoned for a return to power politics, spheres of influence and other discredited and dangerous techniques of the past.

240 This must not be allowed to happen. The United Nations, as a key mechanism for international cooperation by Member States, possesses flexibility, legitimacy and a universal range of action. If employed prudently, efficiently and confidently, the United Nations is the best available instrument for managing the world situation with a reasonable expectation of success.

241 At present this mechanism is caught in a confining cycle. There is a resistance to multilateralism from those who fear a loss of national control. There is a reluctance to provide financial means to achieve agreed ends from those who lack conviction that assessments will benefit their own interests. And there is an unwillingness to engage in difficult operations by those who seek guarantees of perfect clarity and limited duration.

242 Without a new and compelling collective vision, the international community will be unable to break out of this cycle. The present report is, therefore, intended as a first contribution to the search for a revitalized vision of development.

243 In the present report, I have described both the nature and scope of development efforts. I have set out both the dimensions of the development process and the actors involved in it, in the hope that a new vision and culture of development will emerge. Such a vision must, however, be firmly anchored in agreed objectives and commitments on development adopted by the international community, and on a record of demonstrated results, if it is to command sustained support. The United Nations can offer such a record. In addition, the United Nations can bring to bear not only the unparalleled broadness of its scope, but its unique potential to integrate the many actors and dimensions of development.

244 If this promise is to be fulfilled, all organs and entities must perform fully the roles assigned to them by the Charter; roles clearly described but which have yet to be performed entirely as intended.

245 Inspired by the purposes and fundamental principles of the Charter, and mindful of the commitments and objectives adopted by the General Assembly, the international community can now proceed to outline a new vision of development. With the practical commitment of all peoples to the advancement of a new culture of development, the coming celebration of the United Nations first half-century will be marked as a turning-point in the story of all humanity.

Notes

1. Report of the United Nations Conference on Environment and Development, Rio de Janeiro, 3-14 June 1992 *(A/CONF.151/26/Rev.1 (Vol. I and Vol. I/Corr.1, Vol. II and Vol. III and Vol. III/Corr.1)) (United Nations publication, Sales No. E.93.I.8 and corrigenda), vol. I: Resolutions adopted by the Conference, resolution 1, annex II.*

2. A/CONF.157/24 (Part I), chap. III.

3. Official Records of the Third United Nations Conference on the Law of the Sea, vol. XVII *(United Nations publication, Sales No. E.84.V.3), document A/CONF.62/122.*

4. A/AC.237/18 (Part II)/Add.1 and Corr.1, annex I.

ANNEX I

Estimated expenditures on development of the United Nations by organization and by sector, 1992-1993, all sources of funds [a]

(Millions of United States dollars)

Sector	United Nations [b]	UNICEF	UNDP [c]	UNFPA	UNRWA [e]	WFP
General development issues	693.0	48.0	658.1			
General statistics	161.5	11.0	11.1			
Natural resources	119.6		174.5			242.0
Energy	62.3		48.0			
Agriculture, forestry and fisheries	34.7		294.5			342.0
Industry	49.9		147.7			
Transport	47.1		135.1			39.0
Communications	152.1	7.0	21.2			
Trade and development	459.9		58.2			
Population	70.9	8.0	1.7	323.4		
Human settlements	106.3	4.0	101.1			28.0
Health		1,106.0	141.5			209.0
Education		251.0	73.0			296.0
Employment			42.3			
Humanitarian assistance and disaster management	2,518.6	248.0	84.4		601.3	1,850.0
Social development	358.8	124.0	88.5	10.0		
Culture			6.7			
Science and technology	35.3		81.4			
Environment	370.8	3.0	55.5			
Total	**5,240.8**	**1,810.0**	**2,231.5**	**333.4**	**601.3**	**3,006.0**

Source: Report of the Administrative Committee on Coordination (E/1993/84). Explanatory notes on following page.

Explanatory notes to Annex I table

a/ Activities funded by reporting organizations and executed by other reporting organizations are included in the figures for the executing organizations, to avoid double counting.

b/ The figures include data for, *inter alia*, the United Nations Conference on Trade and Development, the United Nations Environment Programme, the United Nations Institute for Training and Research, the United Nations University, the regional commissions, the United Nations Centre for Human Settlements (Habitat), the Office of the United Nations High Commissioner for Refugees and the United Nations Drug Control Programme. The total resources of the International Trade Centre, whose regular budget is financed to the extent of 50 per cent by the General Agreement on Tariffs and Trade (GATT), are also included.

c/ The United Nations Development Programme (UNDP) and the United Nations Population Fund (UNFPA) as funding organizations, provide resources for development. Expenditures are effected through other organizations, directly by UNDP or UNFPA, or through other agents.

UNICEF	United Nations Children's Fund
UNDP	United Nations Development Programme
UNFPA	United Nations Population Fund
UNRWA	United Nations Relief and Works Agency for Palestine Refugees in the Near East
WFP	World Food Programme

ANNEX II

Expenditure on operational activities of the United Nations and its funds and programmes, 1992
(Millions of United States dollars)

1.	Financed by the United Nations Development Programme (UNDP) [a/]	1,026.8
2.	Financed by UNDP-administered funds	137.6
3.	Financed by the United Nations Population Fund (UNFPA)	128.2
4.	Financed by the United Nations Children's Fund (UNICEF)	743.8
5.	Financed by the World Food Programme (WFP) [b/]	1,575.2
6.	Financed by the United Nations regular budget	16.6
	Total [c/]	3,628.2

Source: United Nations, *Progress report of the Secretary-General on the implementation of General Assembly resolution 47/199*, addendum, tables B.1 and B.5 (E/1994/64/Add.2).

a/   That is, UNDP central resources, including expenditures financed from government cost-sharing contributions.

b/   Includes extrabudgetary expenditures by WFP, project expenditures for development activities and emergency operations. Of the latter, most was financed from the International Emergency Food Reserve and the remainder from WFP general resources.

c/   Regular budget financed expenditures of the specialized agencies ($225 million) and their expenditures financed from extrabudgetary sources ($727.2 million) are not included in this total.

ANNEX III

Main United Nations intergovernmental and expert bodies in the economic, social and human rights fields

I. General Assembly and treaty bodies reporting to the assembly

Main Committees	(Second – Economic and Financial; Third – Social, Humanitarian and Cultural)
Treaty bodies	(Elimination of Racial Discrimination; Human Rights – International Covenant on Civil and Political Rights; Economic, Social and Cultural Rights; Elimination of Discrimination against Women; Torture; Rights of the Child)

Total   9 [a/]

II. Economic and Social Council and its subsidiary bodies

Functional commissions	(Statistics; Population; Social Development; Human Rights, including the Subcommission on Prevention of Discrimination and Protection of Minorities; Status of Women; Narcotic Drugs; Science ánd Technology for Development; Sustainable Development; Crime Prevention and Criminal Justice)
Standing and expert bodies	(Transnational Corporations; Human Settlements; New and Renewable Sources of Energy for Development; Non-Governmental Organizations; Programme and Coordination; Natural Resources; Development Planning; Transport of Dangerous Goods; International Cooperation in Tax Matters; Public Administration and Finance; International Standards of Accounting and Reporting; Geographical Names)
Regional commissions	(Economic Commission for Africa; Economic and Social Commission for Asia and the Pacific; Economic Commission for Europe; Economic Commission for Latin America and the Caribbean; Economic and Social Commission for Western Asia)

Total   73 [b/]

III. Other United Nations programmes, organs and funds, and their governing bodies

United Nations Conference
on Trade and Development

Conference
Trade and Development Board, Other
UNCTAD Standing Committees and
Ad Hoc Working Groups (11)

United Nations International
Narcotics Drug Control Programme:

International Control Board

United Nations Development
Programme:

Executive Board

United Nations Environment
Programme:

Governing Council

United Nations Population Fund:

(same board as UNDP)

United Nations High Commissioner
for Refugees:

Executive Committee

United Nations Children's Fund:

Executive Board

United Nations Development
Fund for Women:

Consultative Committee

United Nations Relief and
Works Agency for Palestine
Refugees in the Near East:

Advisory Commission

World Food Council:

World Food Programme:

Committee on Food Aid Policies and
Programmes

	Total	23
	Grand total	105

a/ In addition there are at present preparatory bodies for the World Summit for Social
Development, the Fiftieth Anniversary of the United Nations, the International
Conference on Population and Development, the Global Conference on the
Sustainable Development of Small Island Developing States and the United Nations
Conference on Human Settlements (Habitat II); there are also Intergovernmental
Negotiating Committees for a Framework Convention on Climate Change and for the
Elaboration of an International Convention to Combat Desertification, and a United
Nations Conference on Straddling Fish Stocks and Highly Migratory Fish Stocks.

b/ This total includes 45 subsidiary bodies reporting to the regional commissions.

An Agenda for Development: Recommendations

Report of the Secretary-General
A/49/665, 11 November 1994

Preface

1   IN ACCORDANCE with General Assembly resolution 47/181 of
22 December 1992, I circulated on 6 May 1994 a report on an
Agenda for Development (UN document A/48/935) to elicit the views
of all Member States, the agencies and programmes of the United
Nations system, as well as a wide range of public and private sources.

2   That report was available at the World Hearings on
Development organized by the President of the General Assembly in
June 1994, and was discussed at the substantive session of the
Economic and Social Council in July 1994. Additional comments
were received from a wide variety of sources. I have considered all
contributions with great care. Most recently, I have had the benefit of
statements presented during the general debate of the forty-ninth session of the General Assembly, many of which addressed an agenda
for development.

3   As requested in paragraph 5 of General Assembly resolution
48/166 of 21 December 1993, I am now submitting to the General
Assembly at its forty-ninth session my recommendations, to follow
up on my report on an Agenda for Development of 6 May 1994, taking into account the discussions during the substantive session of
1994 of the Economic and Social Council, as well as the views presented during the Hearings conducted by the President of the General
Assembly and summarized under his own responsibility (UN document A/49/320, annex). In doing so, I have been mindful of the
requests regarding the contents of the Agenda contained in the oper-
ative paragraph of General Assembly resolution 47/181. A summary
of the recommendations appears in the annex to the present report.

I. Introduction

4 The general recommendations that have emerged can be simply stated, but they are fundamentally important. Firstly, development should be recognized as the foremost and most far-reaching task of our time. Recognition of this imperative, commitment to achieving development, and continual, cooperative and effective action towards it are crucial for humanity's common future. It is urgent for Governments, intergovernmental institutions and the United Nations to review their priorities with the goal of elevating dramatically the attention and support given to development.

5 Secondly, development must be seen in its many dimensions. My report on an Agenda for Development of 6 May 1994 identified five dimensions of development: peace, the economy, environmental protection, social justice and democracy. The importance of these dimensions has been understood and supported by Member States. For most people and most countries, economic growth is the *sine qua non* of development. Economic growth is not an option; it is an imperative. But it is a means to an end. New development approaches should not only generate economic growth, they should make its benefits equitably available. They should enable people to participate in decisions affecting their lives. They should provide job-led growth. They must replenish the natural heritage on which all life depends. They must be based upon a comprehensive vision of development.

6 At its core, development must be about improvement of human well-being; removal of hunger, disease and ignorance; and productive employment for all. Its first goal must be to end poverty and satisfy the priority needs of all people in a way that can be productively sustained over future generations.

7 Thirdly, the emerging consensus on the priority and dimensions of development should find expression in a new framework for international cooperation. The enterprise we call international cooperation for development is needed now more than ever, but it must be revitalized in order to escape fully its Cold War past and contribute fully to the realization of development goals.

8 Fourthly, within this new framework for development cooperation, the United Nations must play a major role in both policy leadership and operations. Comments on the May 1994 report on an agenda for development have not only strengthened understanding of the dimensions of development. They have also revealed strong support for a revitalized role of the Organization and for measures to enhance the coherence and relevance of the United Nations system in development.

9 The development mission and responsibilities of the United Nations stem directly from the Charter of the United Nations and the fundamental nature of the United Nations as an international political entity and moral force; from the inseparability of peace-keeping, humanitarian and development objectives; from the contribution of development to the universal goals of peace, freedom, social justice and environmental quality – goals for which the United Nations stands and for which it works daily around the world; and from the strengths of the programmes that have developed over its 50-year life. The United Nations cannot be a strong force for peace unless it is also a strong force for development.

10 It is time for the United Nations to realize its original mandate in the social and economic fields, to make the comprehensive pursuit of development the centre of its action, and, in this new context, to assist Member States in their efforts to realize their diverse development goals.

11 The United Nations system – the United Nations itself, the specialized agencies, and the Bretton Woods institutions – has much to bring to the development process. But the system will realize its potential only if its intergovernmental processes are strengthened and made more coherent and if the various development assistance components integrate their complementary mandates into coherent and coordinated support for countries' aspirations. There is also great room for improvement in the Organization's operations, including the linkages among peace-keeping, humanitarian assistance and development.

12 The general recommendations that have emerged from the process of forging an Agenda for Development have brought to the fore three key objectives: to strengthen and revitalize international development cooperation generally; to build a stronger, more effective and coherent multilateral system in support of development; and to enhance the effectiveness of the development work of the Organization itself – its departments, regional commissions, funds and programmes – in partnership with the United Nations system as a whole.

13   The recommendations presented in the following paragraphs are addressed and organized according to these three objectives, with a special focus in each case on what the United Nations can and should do. No real improvements will be possible unless the Member States are convinced of the need for, and unless nations and peoples everywhere share the fruits of, the proposed changes. Member States are challenged to grasp this opportunity and make the United Nations system a far more effective instrument of multilateralism.

II. Recommendations for revitalizing international development cooperation

14   A new framework for international development cooperation requires mutually supporting actions at the national and international level.

A. National policies for development

15   Development can succeed only if it is driven by national priorities and dedicated to the improvement of the well-being of the country and its people. National capacities to plan, manage and implement development programmes must be built both in government and in civil society.

16   While the individual State is no longer the sole actor in development, each State bears primary responsibility for its own development. Whether expressed as a responsibility of States or as a right of peoples, development requires competent governmental leadership, coherent national policies and strong popular commitment.

17   A strong partnership between government and civil society is an important prerequisite for sustainable development.

18   Governments have a special responsibility to protect poor and marginalized peoples and to seek policies which offer them avenues towards productive involvement in their societies and economies.

19   Non-State actors, including grass-roots people's movements and non-governmental organizations, should be strengthened and supported. These organizations of civil society give a voice to the people, and should be recognized and included in new development models.

20   The importance of private business should not be underestimated. As part of the partnership, strong private enterprise sectors, the use of market forces and market-based mechanisms, and the cultivation of entrepreneurship should be encouraged. Governments should ensure that social and environmental costs are accurately reflected in prices, and lead to macroeconomic stability.

21   Government, civil and social action must be taken to fight corruption and protect consumers, investors, workers and the environment through appropriate regulations.

B. International setting

22   A favourable, growth-oriented international setting for development is vital. External macroeconomic forces – trade, debt management, direct investment, capital flows and access to technology – must support development objectives. International cooperation for development must include partnerships with the business community, national and international.

23   The equitable integration of the poorest and least-endowed countries into the world economy is a major requirement. The marginalization of these countries is perceptible and must be reversed.

24   It is distressing that the official development assistance target of 0.7 per cent of gross national product, which was adopted in 1970 and reaffirmed as recently as 1992 at the United Nations Conference on Environment and Development (UNCED), was achieved in 1993 by only four countries: Denmark, the Netherlands, Norway and Sweden. Development assistance must be brought closer to the agreed targets, and its diversion to non-development priorities must be reversed. New agreements should be reached on plausible interim goals for steady increases in official development assistance. A larger share should be allocated to the development work of the United Nations.

25 There is an urgent need to increase the overall level of development assistance and to ensure that funding for peace-keeping, humanitarian emergencies and the global environment is provided from new and additional resources and not from development assistance.

26 The international community must find a solution for an issue that has bedevilled development efforts for two decades: debt. Debt problems are acute among the poorest countries, particularly those in Africa.

27 Reforming countries in debt crisis require an adequate and permanent reduction in the stock of debt that will restore private sector confidence at home and abroad and facilitate their recovery, growth and development. The debts of the least developed and poorest countries should be cancelled outright. Recycling debt to finance economic, social and environmental projects should be considered.

28 Developing nations must be provided equitable access to expanding global opportunities in trade, technology, investment and information. The fruits of the technological and informatics revolution must be more evenly available if present international economic disparities are not to deepen further and weaken the foundations of global progress.

29 Countries in transition to a market economy face special problems stemming from the need for rapid but sensitive transformation in fundamental economic organization, lack of competitiveness in international markets, economic depression and other factors. These countries should be supported by additional resources from the international community.

30 Regional economic cooperation should be recognized as an important component of many countries' development strategies. Regional integration schemes, from loose associations to free trade agreements, provide a rich experience upon which new policy initiatives can draw. Economic and technical cooperation among developing countries with similar challenges and experiences should be encouraged.

31   Economic progress and human well-being in many parts of the world are threatened by unchecked population growth and environmental deterioration. Programmes to address these issues, including the Programme of Action recently forged at the International Conference on Population and Development in Cairo and the agreements reached at UNCED in Rio de Janeiro, must be given high priority as an integral part of comprehensive development.

32   The rapid application of new technology and changes in consumption are needed to check extravagant consumption of natural and environmental resources.

33   Excessive military spending and its consequences are deeply inimical to development goals. A unique opportunity is now available for further progress on reducing military expenditures, phasing out most forms of military assistance and subsidies to arms exporters, and effectively curtailing indiscriminate international trafficking in arms. Greater transparency of military spending is needed. The United Nations Register of Conventional Arms must be strengthened. More extensive comparative analysis of military and social budgets must be undertaken. Land-mines are a major obstacle to development, shattering lives and removing land from productive use. An outright worldwide ban on the production and transfer of land-mines and their components should be declared. The holding of world hearings on the connection between disarmament and development conducted by the President of the General Assembly should be seriously considered.

34   As the success of the International Conference on Population and Development at Cairo demonstrates, a powerful international development agenda is emerging on an ongoing basis through the work of a continuum of United Nations conferences and summits. Effective and realistic mechanisms must be made available to implement goals established at these conferences.

35   A common framework should be developed to follow up major United Nations conferences, past and future. Goals and targets in the economic and social development field endorsed by past international conferences and summits should be synthesized, costed, prioritized and placed in a reasonable time perspective for implementation.

36   The fiftieth session of the General Assembly provides an appropriate opportunity for focusing the attention of the international community on forging a new framework for development cooperation between industrialized and developing countries, in which common interests and mutual needs provide the basic rationale for a new partnership.

37   In this regard, an international conference on the financing of development should be considered by the Assembly. Such a conference could be convened in close consultation with the Bretton Woods institutions, the regional development banks and the Development Assistance Committee of the Organization for Economic Cooperation and Development.

III. Recommendations for an effective multilateral development system

38   With increasing global interdependence, the need for multilateral cooperation will inevitably expand. A strong and effective multilateral system with the United Nations at its centre is an essential prerequisite for successful multilateral cooperation on development and international economic policy and operations.

39   The responsibility for building a new framework for development cooperation is widely shared. But the role of the United Nations is unique and indispensable. As the world Organization based on the principle of universality, and with an unmatched global network at all levels, the United Nations can promote awareness, build consensus, inform policy in every dimension affecting development, and help to rationalize and harmonize the multiplicity of public and private efforts worldwide in the cause of development. Enhancing the role of the General Assembly and the Economic and Social Council, and strengthening linkages between the Organization and the Bretton Woods institutions on the one hand, and the sectoral and technical agencies on the other, are crucial requirements to these ends.

A. *General Assembly*

40 In the context of the ongoing intergovernmental reform process on the restructuring and revitalization of the United Nations in the economic, social and related fields, the General Assembly must play a major role to focus the attention of the international community on forging a new framework for development cooperation.

41 The General Assembly should identify critical issues for international cooperation and policy development and serve as a forum for regular identification of gaps and inconsistencies, as well as emerging problems that are likely to fall between the purviews of more narrowly focused institutions in the fields of development, trade and finance. The Assembly should focus on the development of norms, standards and rules of the game required to manage global interdependence in a rapidly changing international environment and promote an integrated approach to economic and social development. The roles of the Second and Third Committees could be reviewed from this perspective.

42 The early part of General Assembly sessions, with high-level representatives present, could be used to organize a focused dialogue on these issues in the plenary sessions. Consideration could be given to convening, every few years, special sessions of the Assembly on major aspects of international cooperation for development.

B. *Economic and Social Council*

43 Key to the ongoing effort to strengthen the United Nations as the centre of an effective multilateral development system is the revitalization of the Economic and Social Council to fulfil the role envisaged for it under the Charter.

44 Firstly, the Council should deliberate and decide upon the full range of development issues in accordance with that role, mindful of the Relationship Agreements with and mandates of the specialized agencies and the Bretton Woods institutions. The Council should bring the specialized agencies into a closer working relationship with the United Nations and perform the functions specified in the Charter under Chapter IV, on the General Assembly; Chapter IX, on international economic and social cooperation; and Chapter X, on the Council itself.

45   Secondly, the Council should serve as an international development assistance review committee, providing a regular opportunity for both donors and recipients to discuss and assess aid programmes and policies. As part of this role, the Council should function as a unifying governing entity to which the existing governing bodies of the United Nations funds and programmes would relate on major policy matters. It would also provide intergovernmental oversight of the relevant United Nations departments with responsibilities for operational activities for development.

46   Thirdly, the Council should identify potential or emerging humanitarian emergencies and provide policy guidelines in developing coordinated initiatives to address such situations.

47   These responsibilities and functions of the Council could be reinforced by an expanded bureau, meeting inter-sessionally to focus the work of the Council and facilitate agreement on issues for endorsement by the Council. To preserve efficiency while retaining representativeness, the expanded bureau should be limited in membership. Its working methods should provide for maximum flexibility so as to ensure timely responses. The entire Council, at a high level, would meet at specific times of the year to provide general policy guidance and to review the work of the expanded bureau.

48   To support the General Assembly and the Economic and Social Council in providing effective leadership in development, a council of international development advisers should be considered. This council would issue an independent annual or biennial report, analyse key issues concerning the global economy and their impact on development, and inform international opinion.

C. Bretton Woods institutions

49   Strengthening the links with the Bretton Woods institutions was one of the dominant themes during the recent debate in the Economic and Social Council high-level session and in the World

Hearings on Development. Enhancing the relationship between the United Nations and the Bretton Woods institutions is one of the mandates contained in the original General Assembly resolution 47/181 calling for an Agenda for Development.

50   There are many fields in which the ongoing dialogue and substantive partnerships between the Bretton Woods institutions and the United Nations may be strengthened. In particular, with the expansion of the World Bank lending into social, environmental and other sectors which require capacity building, decentralized planning and execution, small loans and more participatory development involving all institutions of civil society, there should be greater scope for collaboration with United Nations programmes and agencies working in these areas.

51   Similarly, the World Bank could utilize and support United Nations programmes in delivering grant-based technical assistance, particularly "free standing" technical assistance unrelated to specific capital investment projects.

52   There are successful examples of country-level collaboration between the Bretton Woods institutions and the United Nations programmes in these and other areas, which should be employed as models for replication.

53   Cooperation between the Bretton Woods institutions and the United Nations could be pursued through joint initiatives in, among others, the following fields: poverty reduction strategies, including small enterprise development and micro-credit availability; improvements in the productivity of the resources sector and sustainable energy development; preventive development and post-conflict peace-building and reconstruction; socially and environmentally responsible structural adjustment programmes; and capacity-building and improved public sector management.

54   An issue that has attracted considerable attention in the Economic and Social Council discussions and in the World Hearings on Development is the policy conditionality for structural adjustment loans designed by the World Bank and the International Monetary Fund (IMF). There is little disagreement on the need for structural

adjustment and economic reform. There is, however, controversy over the policy content of structural adjustment programmes and concern that such programmes are, in and of themselves, insufficient.

55   The Organization and the Bretton Woods institutions should work together with concerned countries on the components of the policy dialogue and other complementary and compensating initiatives that must accompany structural adjustment programmes. There is considerable scope for such collaboration in the aid consortia, consultative groups and round tables organized under multilateral auspices, particularly by the World Bank and the United Nations Development Programme (UNDP). Special attention also needs to be given to making the country policy dialogue more transparent and relevant by building Governments' capacities to lead the dialogue process and in clearly detailing policy options in country documents prepared by the World Bank/IMF and the United Nations development system. The United Nations resident coordinator should be involved with such policy dialogues. Efforts now under way to promote greater complementarity between country strategy notes and policy framework papers should be pursued.

56   The revival of the United Nations/Bretton Woods Liaison Committee could also be explored with the aim of enhancing substantive consultation. In addition, the Secretary-General should convey, as appropriate, the concerns of the United Nations system as a whole to the Joint Committee on Development of the Board of Governors of the IMF and the World Bank.

D. Sectoral and technical agencies

57   The diversity represented in the agencies of the United Nations system can be a great source of strength if the variety of constituencies and expertise which they represent is harnessed in support of comprehensive, sustainable development.

58   The contribution which the sectoral and technical agencies have been making to the preparation for, and follow-up to, major global conferences – encompassing intergovernmental policy inputs, specialized secretariat expertise, and the promotion of contributions

from different sectors of civil society – represents a model which should be applied progressively to all aspects of the development work of the Organization. Initiatives for joint action, such as the new inter-agency programme on the human immunodeficiency virus/acquired immunodeficiency syndrome (HIV/AIDS), should similarly be expanded to other areas.

59 Technical contributions from these agencies, particularly the smaller technical agencies concerned with various aspects of infrastructure development, should be integrated more fully in economic and social plans and priorities promoted by the United Nations system.

60 Maintaining the integrity and comprehensive nature of the United Nations system should be a major, constant concern of the international community. In this context, the desirability of bringing new organizations such as the World Trade Organization, endowed with wide international responsibilities in fields of international economic and social cooperation, into relationship with the United Nations, deserves priority attention.

61 In line with the objectives that have guided the recent restructuring of the inter-secretariat coordination machinery, members of the Administrative Committee on Coordination, under the chairmanship of the Secretary-General, will pursue further measures to strengthen the contribution of that Committee to enhancing the coherence and impact of the work of the system. As part of this effort, it is intended to make greater use of small task forces at the executive head level focusing on critical development issues, and to develop joint programmes based on common policies for implementation at the country level.

IV. Recommendations for more efficient and effective United Nations development activities

62 The development activities of the Organization span a wide range: long-term social, economic and political development; post-crisis reconstruction and rehabilitation; and issues such as population, the status of women, child survival, the environment, drug control, and housing and urban management. Confidence in the United Nations depends to a large extent on the efficiency and effectiveness of these programmes.

63   The fundamental reason for improving United Nations development assistance efforts is not because these efforts are failing but because they are succeeding. The demand for the services that the United Nations provides far outstrips its capacity. In other words, the need to build on past successes, to take full advantage of proven capabilities and to respond to new demands and new opportunities, is the most compelling reason for strengthening United Nations operational activities for development.

64   Further measures to improve and strengthen governance, management, funding, the division of labour and the allocation of responsibilities, coordination and staffing, must build upon the reform initiatives undertaken to date. These include the series of changes in United Nations operations set in motion by General Assembly resolutions 44/211 of 22 December 1989 and 47/199 of 22 December 1992, in the context of its triennial policy reviews of operational activities for development, as well as by other restructuring and revitalization efforts. Enhancing coordination and effectiveness within the United Nations itself can go a long way to foster coherence in the system as a whole.

A. Assets and strengths

65   Efforts to make United Nations operational activities more efficient and effective must begin with careful identification of those areas where the United Nations has special assets and strengths in support of development.

66   The United Nations provides a unique forum for raising public consciousness, providing information, defining the international development agenda and building the consensus needed for action. Once forged, consensus is translated into international norms and agreements, integrated into national development priorities and supported through United Nations operational activities.

67   The neutrality of the United Nations means that it does not

represent any particular national or commercial interest. The United Nations can therefore develop special relationships of trust with the countries it supports in their development efforts. It can provide stable, long-term capacity-building assistance free of short-term political or economic objectives.

68   The United Nations has an unmatched global network of regional commissions and country offices. The resulting delivery capacity of the United Nations is uniquely strong. Because of its universal presence, the United Nations can operate effectively at both the country and the intercountry and regional levels.

69   The United Nations emphasizes bottom-up, country-driven programming of development assistance resources, without conditionalities. Coupled with the participation of developing countries in United Nations governance, this ensures that United Nations development initiatives derive from national priorities and are dedicated to the progress of the countries involved and their peoples.

70   The United Nations has a comprehensive mandate, spanning social, economic and political issues. Working in partnership with the specialized agencies, the United Nations has expertise across virtually the full range of development interests. This breadth further enhances delivery capacity.

71   United Nations programmes focus on the neediest countries and on the neediest people within those countries. The United Nations has special strengths and experience in addressing social aspects of development and integrating social and economic dimensions, working with Governments, grass-roots people's movements and other non-governmental organizations.

72   The United Nations is able to mobilize, deliver and coordinate humanitarian assistance. It can promote reconstruction, reintegration and other development in post-emergency situations. It can link peace-keeping, refugee assistance, relief efforts and development. It provides an ideal base for support for early warning and preventive development initiatives. In this area, as in others, the United Nations organizations have established close working relationships with non-governmental organizations at all levels.

B. Common goals

73   Where there is a shared vision and common purpose, coordination and integration in the Organization's operational activities will follow. Through international conferences and in other ways, the United Nations and its Member States are seeking to articulate and promote a shared vision of development that is human-centred, equitable, and socially and environmentally sustainable. Through this process, common goals are emerging that can serve to galvanize the energies and focus the efforts of the United Nations funds and programmes, together with their agency partners.

74   A major goal in this regard is the empowerment of women. With the emerging consensus on the priority and dimensions of development has come a deeper understanding that in virtually every dimension of development – whether political, social, economic, environmental or security related – the role of women is central. Policies and institutions that suppress the real potential of half of the Earth's people must be reformed. The empowerment of women must be recognized and utilized as a powerful tool for liberating the full creative energies of a society. The visibility, coordination, programming and accountability of the United Nations in gender-related development issues must be improved.

75   The outcome of the International Conference on Population and Development, the adoption of the Declaration on the Elimination of Violence against Women by the General Assembly at its forty-eighth session, and the decision of the Commission on Human Rights to create the position of the Special Rapporteur on violence against women are major recent achievements for the protection of women's human rights. At the Fourth World Conference on Women, further international agreement on measures to promote the advancement of women should be reached. Implementation of such agreements should proceed in a coordinated way and be fully integrated in overall development efforts.

76   Three other common goals are outlined in the paragraphs that follow: poverty eradication, preventive and curative development, and African development. Member States are urged to support United

Nations leadership in these areas. Other key goals that can unify the development work of the United Nations funds and programmes range from support for programme country priorities in food security, full employment and education for all, to protecting and regenerating the natural resource base for sustained production.

77   All countries should agree on a global compact to eliminate poverty over a specified period of time.

78   Upcoming conferences, especially the World Summit for Social Development and the Fourth World Conference on Women, can define clear, ambitious and monitorable objectives in the area of poverty eradication, supported by operational strategies adapted to each country's situation. The United Nations should play a direct role in this effort to seek to mobilize action on these objectives by the entire international community.

79   The critical elements for a poverty eradication initiative – such as basic social services, employment generation, food security, drug and transnational crime control, and access to credit, technology, training and markets – should be integrated into a comprehensive operational package.

80   Recent years have witnessed phenomenal growth in the Organization's activities in peace-keeping, refugee assistance and other humanitarian relief. These activities must be complemented by new development initiatives for preventive and curative development.

81   Preventive development is a necessary complement to preventive diplomacy. The United Nations should build state-of-the-art capabilities to act preventively for development, anticipating and responding to crises, natural and man-made, before they occur. As proposed earlier, this should be a new main focus of the work of the Economic and Social Council.

82   A global watch system should be considered to provide early detection of impending humanitarian emergencies and guidelines for preventive action for consideration by the Economic and Social Council. This system would access, build upon and seek to strengthen existing capabilities.

83   A new focus on curative development is required. When the

time comes to heal the wounds of a society, demobilize soldiers and reintegrate refugees and internally displaced persons, timely, post-conflict peace-building and development – including reconstruction and rehabilitation – are essential.

84 Special initiatives to give added momentum to development efforts in Africa are urgently required. Of the 47 least developed countries in the world, 33 are in Africa. Africa accounts for just 2 per cent of world trade and only 1.4 per cent of world exports. Economic growth is hampered by external debt problems, by the decrease in external resource flows, by sharply declining terms of trade and by mounting barriers to market access. Desertification poses a severe obstacle to development. And across the continent, the persistence of poverty and widespread unemployment have undermined social con-fidence and social stability, fuelling conflict and unrest.

85 In the light of Economic and Social Council resolution 1994/38 of 29 July 1994 on the United Nations New Agenda for the Development of Africa in the 1990s, and as suggested in the most recent meeting of the Administrative Committee on Coordination, consideration is being given to setting up a task force of that Committee to identify major inter-agency initiatives to be taken in support of Africa. The task force would focus on the development of country-level cooperation around specific goals and issues and define the required policy options to galvanize international support for African economic recovery and development.

C. Operational coordination

86 The various development entities comprising the United Nations have their own organizational cultures, public name recogni-tion and constituencies, and resource mobilization capacities. Moreover, a certain amount of organizational diversity and pluralism can be healthy. Efforts to enhance operational coordination within the United Nations should endeavour to achieve the benefits of a uni-fied system, while preserving the strength of the current approach.

87 Such efforts should be aimed at the following objectives, among others: building a more integrated, efficient and effective framework through which the United Nations can better assist countries in realizing their development objectives, including clearer and more complementary definition of the roles and missions of the various components; eliminating duplication and fragmentation; strengthening leadership and cooperation at country, regional and headquarters levels; strengthening United Nations capabilities in the coordination and delivery of humanitarian assistance, the linking of emergency relief and development, and the promotion of preventive and curative development; mobilizing analytical and normative capacities and strengthening the role of the Organization in interrelated areas such as trade and access to technology, in support of operational activities; defining the appropriate level – country, region or headquarters – for activity on various issues; integrating the regional commissions with the development work of the Organization as a whole; strengthening the resident coordinator and country-driven approaches; streamlining the delivery capacity of the United Nations through common premises, the programme approach and common programming cycles; and achieving more rapid and aggressive implementation of General Assembly resolutions 44/211 and 47/199, including the country strategy note and other tools, for a more integrated United Nations response to country priorities.

88   In pursuit of these objectives, I intend to convene frequent meetings of all senior officials in the economic and social sector, with the support of the Administrator of UNDP, as a main instrument to improve overall programme coordination and policy coherence within the Organization. The outcome of the work of a strengthened Joint Consultative Group on Policy, focusing on country-level coordination and related issues, should constitute an important input into these senior official meetings.

89   When operational activities for development are undertaken within the context of a peace-keeping mission, which is placed under the command of a special representative, all elements of the United Nations system at all levels that are active in the theatre of operations must come under the command and direction of the special representative. It must be recognized that the special representative has not only a political but also an essential coordinating role in this regard.

D. Financing for the future

90   Although better operational coordination and a top-calibre international civil service are essential, the effectiveness of the United Nations operational activities for development will ultimately depend upon financial resources. The most significant difficulty facing the United Nations entities engaged in development work is that they are unable, owing to resource constraints, to mount assistance efforts on a scale commensurate with the challenges they help Member States address.

91.   The United Nations is in financial crisis. Reliance on voluntary contributions alone, in light of the expanded development mandate of the Organization, is no longer feasible. To deal with this, a number of principles and proposals have been put forward. It has been recognized that more resources are needed, that mandates and the resources provided for them must be in a sound relationship, and that predictability in funding is essential so that operations are not undermined in the midst of performance. It has been suggested that a system of assessed, negotiated and voluntary contributions provides the most logical and appropriate means of financing the United Nations as it permits Governments to maintain proper control over the United Nations' budget and its agenda. It has further been suggested that the Organization should review its voluntarily funded programmes, especially those that are financed through trust funds, to eliminate unnecessary and duplicative expenditures. Other measures that may be considered include a fee on speculative international financial transactions, a levy on fossil fuel use (or its resulting pollution) in all countries, earmarking a small portion of the anticipated decline in world military expenditures, utilizing some of the resources that could be released through the elimination of unnecessary subsidies, and utilizing resources generated from a stamp tax on international travel and travel documents.

V. Conclusion

92.   The battle for people-centred and sustainable development will be won or lost not in the corridors of Governments, but in every hamlet and home, in every village and town, in the daily enterprise of every member of the global community and every institution of civil society. The Charter of the United Nations begins with a pledge by "We the Peoples ...". It is the people, on whose behalf we all act, who are the true custodians of the emerging new vision of development. It is for them that we must work to achieve a new framework for development cooperation and the revitalization of the United Nations system.

ANNEX
An Agenda for Development: key recommendations

Development must be driven by national priorities. Through a partnership involving government, civil society and strong private enterprise sectors, national capacities to plan, manage and implement development programmes must be built.

External macroeconomic forces must support development objectives. Developing countries must be provided equitable access to expanding global opportunities in trade, technology, investment and information.

Development assistance must be brought closer to the agreed targets. New agreements should be reached on plausible interim goals for steady increases in official development assistance and a larger share should be allocated to the development work of the United Nations.

An adequate and permanent reduction in the stock of debt for countries in debt crisis undertaking economic reforms should be made. The debts of the least developed and poorest countries should be cancelled outright.

Countries in transition to market economies should be supported by additional resources from the international community.

Further progress must be made on reducing military expenditures. Hearings by the President of the General Assembly on the connection between disarmament and development may be considered.

A common framework should be developed to implement goals established in United Nations conferences. Goals and targets should be synthesized, costed, prioritized and placed in a reasonable time perspective for implementation.

The fiftieth session of the General Assembly should focus the attention of the international community on forging a new framework for development cooperation. In that context, the desirability of an international conference on the financing of development should also be considered.

An effective multilateral development system requires that the unique role of the United Nations be recognized and supported: its universality, unmatched network, and capacity to build consensus, inform policy, and help rationalize public and private development efforts.

The General Assembly should identify critical issues and serve as a forum for emerging problems that fall between the purviews of more narrowly focused institutions in development, trade and finance. It should focus on requirements for a more effective management of global interdependence and the promotion of an integrated approach to economic and social development.

The early part of General Assembly sessions, with high-level representatives present, could focus dialogue on development issues in the plenary sessions. Special sessions on major aspects of international cooperation for development should be considered.

The Economic and Social Council must be revitalized to fulfil the role envisaged in the Charter. A revitalized Council should:

- bring specialized agencies into a closer working relationship with the United Nations; serve as an international development assistance review committee, and function as a unifying governing entity to which the governing bodies of the United Nations funds and programmes would relate; and identify impending humanitarian emergencies and provide policy guidelines for coordinated initiatives.

Consideration should be given to an expanded bureau of the Council, meeting inter-sessionally, to facilitate agreement on issues for endorsement by the Council.

Greater cooperation between the United Nations and the Bretton Woods institutions should be pursued through joint initiatives, such as:

- poverty reduction strategies, sustainable energy development, post-conflict peace-building, capacity-building and improved public sector management.

The Organization and the Bretton Woods institutions should work together with concerned countries on the components of the policy dialogue and other initiatives that must accompany structural adjustment programmes. Governments' capacities to lead the dialogue process must be reinforced, with the support of the Resident Coordinator. Greater complementarity of country documents should be pursued.

The contributions of technical and sectoral agencies should be integrated more fully in development strategies, in support of comprehensive, sustainable development.

The integrity and comprehensive nature of the United Nations system must be maintained. Bringing new organizations such as the World Trade Organization into relationship with the United Nations deserves priority attention.

Members of the Administrative Committee on Coordination, under the chairmanship of the Secretary-General, will pursue further measures to strengthen the coherence and impact of the work of the United Nations system.

Further measures to improve governance, management, funding, and allocation of responsibilities, coordination and staffing, must build upon reform initiatives undertaken to date, including changes set in motion by General Assembly resolutions 44/211 and 47/199, as well as other restructuring and revitalization efforts.

The empowerment of women, poverty eradication, preventive and curative development, and special initiatives to support African development, are crucial areas in which the United Nations should provide leadership and focus action. Other key goals which can unify the development work of the United Nations include food, security, full employment, education for all, and protecting and regenerating the natural resource base for sustained production.

Efforts to enhance operational coordination should endeavour to achieve the benefits of a unified system, while preserving the strength of the current approach. Among the objectives should be:

- a more integrated, efficient, and effective structure for United Nations development assistance; strengthening United Nations capabilities in the coordination and delivery of humanitarian assistance; mobilizing the analytical role of the Organization in interrelated areas such as trade and access to technology in support of operations; integrating the regional commissions with the development work of the Organization; strengthening the Resident Coordinator and country-driven approaches for a more integrated United Nations response to country priorities.

To these ends, the Secretary-General will convene frequent meetings of all senior officials for the economic and social sectors with the support of the Administrator of UNDP.

In peace-keeping operations, all elements of the United Nations system at all levels undertaking development activities as part of the mission must come under the command and direction of the Special Representative in command of that mission.

United Nations development efforts must be supported by adequate financial resources. Reliance on voluntary contributions alone, in light of the expanded development mandate of the Organization, is no longer feasible.

Three principles are fundamental: more resources are needed; mandates and the resources provided for them must be in a sound relationship; and predictability in funding is essential so that operations are not undermined in the midst of performance.

Section Two
RELATED
UN DOCUMENTS

LIST OF REPRODUCED DOCUMENTS

Resolutions of the General Assembly

An Agenda for Development
A/RES/47/181, 22 December 1992

The General Assembly,

Recalling the Charter of the United Nations, in particular the commitment to employ international machinery for the promotion of the economic and social advancement of all peoples,

Taking note of the report of the Secretary-General on the work of the Organization, in particular the reference to an agenda for development,[1/*]

Reaffirming the unique position of the United Nations as a forum for the promotion of international cooperation for development,

Emphasizing the need to give due consideration to the broad scope of themes related to international cooperation and international economic relations in order to address effectively the issue of development, particularly of developing countries,

Stressing the importance of continuing to strengthen the capacity of the United Nations to foster international cooperation in order to address fully the wide range of issues pertaining to development, particularly that of developing countries,

Stressing also that the objectives and commitments with regard to development adopted by the General Assembly, especially the Declaration on International Economic Cooperation, in particular the Revitalization of Economic Growth and Development of the Developing Countries,[2/] the International Development Strategy for the Fourth United Nations Development Decade,[3/] the Cartagena Commitment,[4/] the United Nations New Agenda for the Development of Africa in the 1990s,[5/] the Programme of Action for the Least Developed Countries for the 1990s,[6/] and the various consensus agreements and conventions, especially Agenda 21, adopted by the United Nations Conference on Environment and Development[7/] at the level of heads of State or Government, which mark the beginning of a new

---

global partnership for sustainable development, all together provide the overall framework of international cooperation for development,

Recalling the restructuring and revitalization process initiated by its resolution 45/264 of 13 May 1991, in particular its commitment to promote the achievement of the objectives and priorities of the United Nations in the economic, social and related fields, as set forth in other relevant resolutions,

Requests the Secretary-General to submit to the General Assembly at its forty-eighth session, in consultation with Member States, a report on an agenda for development, taking fully into consideration the objectives and agreements on development adopted by the Assembly, containing an analysis of and recommendations on ways to enhance the role of the United Nations and the relationship between the United Nations and the Bretton Woods institutions in the promotion of international cooperation for development, within the framework and provisions of the Charter of the United Nations and the articles of agreement of the Bretton Woods institutions, and to include therein, *inter alia*, a comprehensive annotated list of substantive themes and areas to be addressed by the United Nations in the agenda, as well as his views on priorities among them, for the consideration of Member States.

1/ Official Records of the General Assembly, Forty-seventh Session, Supplement No. 1 *(A/47/1), para. 105.*

2/ *Resolution S-18/3, annex.*

3/ *Resolution 45/199.*

4/ *See* Report of the United Nations Conference on Trade and Development on its Eighth Session, Cartagena de Indias, Colombia, 8-25 February 1992 *(TD/364), part one, sect. A.*

5/ *Resolution 46/151, annex, sect. 11.*

6/ *See* Report of the Second United Nations Conference on the Least Developed Countries, Paris, 3-14 September 1990 *(A/CONF.147/18), part one.*

7/ *See* Report of the United Nations Conference on Environment and Davelopment, Rio de Janeiro, 3-14 June 1992 *(A/CONF.151/26, vols. I, II and Corr.1, and III).47/182.*

An Agenda for Development
A/RES/48/166, 21 December 1993

The General Assembly,

Recalling its resolution 47/181 of 22 December 1992,

Convinced of the need to elaborate a framework to promote international consensus in the field of development,

Committed to strengthening the effectiveness of the United Nations in the economic and social sectors, and recognizing, in this respect, the need to revive the role of the United Nations in fostering and promoting international cooperation for economic and social development,

Taking note of the views expressed by States on an agenda for development,

Welcoming the intention of the Secretary-General to issue in the early months of 1994 the report requested in its resolution 47/181,

1. *Takes note with appreciation* of the note by the Secretary-General on progress in the implementation of General Assembly resolution 47/181;[1/]

2. *Decides* that the intergovernmental discussions to consider an agenda for development and the reports of the Secretary-General thereon should be held at the substantive session of 1994 of the Economic and Social Council and at the forty-ninth session of the General Assembly;

3. *Invites* the President of the General Assembly to promote, as early as possible in 1994, in an open-ended format, broad-based discussions and an exchange of views on an agenda for development, on the basis of the report of the Secretary-General requested in its resolution 47/181;

4. *Also invites* the President of the General Assembly, in order to ensure the broad-based nature of those discussions, to invite relevant programmes, funds and agencies of the United Nations system, relevant multilateral institutions and other relevant organizations, including scientific and academic institutions, to participate

fully in or present their views during those discussions;

5. *Requests* the Secretary-General to submit to the General Assembly at its forty-ninth session further recommendations, as appropriate, to follow up his report on an agenda for development, taking into account the views expressed during the substantive session of 1994 of the Economic and Social Council, as well as the views expressed during the discussions promoted by the President of the General Assembly and summarized under his own responsibility;

6. *Recommends* that the Economic and Social Council, at its organizational session for 1994, consider "An agenda for development" as a possible topic for the high-level segment of its substantive session of 1994;

7. *Decides* to hold special plenary meetings at a high level, at its forty-ninth session, to consider ways of promoting and giving political impetus to an agenda for development;

8. *Also decides* to include in the provisional agenda of its forty-ninth session an item entitled "An agenda for development".

1/ *A/48/689.*

An Agenda for Development
A/RES/49/126, 19 December 1994

The General Assembly,

Recalling its resolutions 47/181 of 22 December 1992 and 48/166 of 21 December 1993,

Taking note of the reports submitted by the Secretary-General on an Agenda for Development,[1]

Welcoming the World Hearings on Development promoted by the President of the forty-eighth session of the General Assembly, and convened in New York from 6 to 10 June 1993, which provided a substantive contribution to the ongoing debates on an Agenda for Development, and taking note of the note by the President of the forty-eighth session of the Assembly and his summary of the World Hearings on Development,[2]

Noting the debates held within the high-level segment of the substantive session of 1994 of the Economic and Social Council, and taking note of the summary and conclusions of the President of the Council,[3]

Underlining its commitment to the elaboration of an action-oriented consensual framework to promote international cooperation for development and to strengthen the role of the United Nations in the economic and social sectors,

1. *Decides* to establish an ad hoc open-ended working group of the General Assembly to elaborate further an action-oriented, comprehensive Agenda for Development, which should begin its work as early as possible in 1995;

2. *Requests* the ad hoc open-ended working group of the General Assembly, in its deliberations to take into account the reports, and the recommendations presented by the Secretary-General pursuant to Assembly resolutions 47/181 and 48/166; the outcome of the high-level segment of the substantive session of 1994 of the Economic and Social Council, the views expressed by representatives in the high-level debate held during the present session of the Assembly, as well as the summary of the World Hearings on Development,[2] and proposals presented by groups and/or States, including the convening of a UN conference on development;

3.   *Requests* the Economic and Social Council, at its organizational session for 1995, to consider ways and means for the Council to give further substantive input to the work of the ad hoc working group;

4.   *Requests* the ad hoc open-ended working group to consider appropriate modalities for the finalization and adoption of an Agenda for Development;

5.   *Also requests* the ad hoc open-ended working group to submit a report on the progress of its work to the Assembly before the conclusion of its present session;

6.   *Decides* to include in the provisional agenda of its fiftieth session the item entitled "Agenda for Development".

1/   *A/48/689, A/48/935 and A/49/665.*

2/   *A/49/320, annex.*

3/   *E/1994/109.*

Report of the Economic and Social Council

High-Level Segment of the Council
A/49/3 (Chapter II), 12 September 1994

1. At its organizational session for 1994, the Council decided:
(a) That the high-level segment should be devoted to the consideration of the following major theme: "An agenda for development";
(b) That the high-level segment with ministerial participation should be held from 27 to 29 June 1994 (decision 1994/201).

2. Pursuant to General Assembly resolution 45/264, the high-level segment was open to all Member States in accordance with Article 69 of the Charter of the United Nations.

A. Proceedings of the high-level segment

3. The high-level segment was held from 27 to 29 June 1994 (9th to 15th meetings of the Council). An account of the proceedings is contained in the relevant summary records (E/1994/SR.9-15). The Council had before it the following documents:
(a) Report of the Secretary-General on an agenda for development (A/48/935);
(b) Letter dated 27 June 1994 from the Permanent Representative of Algeria to the United Nations addressed to the Secretary-General transmitting the Ministerial Statement on an agenda for development, adopted by the Group of 77 on 24 June 1994 (A/49/204-E/1994/90);
(c) Letter dated 27 June 1994 from the Permanent Representative of Algeria to the United Nations addressed to the Secretary-General transmitting the Ministerial Statement adopted on the occasion of the thirtieth anniversary of the Group of 77 (A/49/205-E/1994/91);

(d) Letter dated 29 June 1994 from the Chargé d'affaires a.i. of the Permanent Mission of Yugoslavia to the United Nations addressed to the Secretary-General (E/1994/101).

4.   At the 9th meeting of the Council, on 27 June, the President of the Council made a statement.

5.   At the same meeting, the Council began its policy dialogue and discussion on important developments in the world economy and international economic cooperation with the heads of multilateral financial and trade institutions of the United Nations system.

6.   Statements were made by the President of the World Bank, the Managing Director of the International Monetary Fund, the Officer-in-charge of the United Nations Conference on Trade and Development and the Deputy Director-General of the General Agreement on Tariffs and Trade.

7.   During the exchange of views, statements were made by the representatives of the United States of America, Belgium, Germany, Norway and Greece.

8.   The President of the World·Bank, the Managing Director of the International Monetary Fund, the Officer-in-charge of the United Nations Conference on Trade and Development, the Deputy Director-General of the General Agreement on Tariffs and Trade and the Under-Secretary-General for Policy Coordination and Sustainable Development responded to questions raised during the exchange of views.

9.   At the 10th meeting, on 27 June, the Council continued its policy dialogue. During the exchange of views, statements were made by the representatives of Denmark, India, Egypt, the Russian Federation, Nigeria, Chile, China, the United Kingdom of Great Britain and Northern Ireland, Bangladesh, Japan, Indonesia and Belarus and the observers for Algeria and Morocco.

10. The observer for the European Community also made a statement.

11. The Managing Director of the International Monetary Fund, the Officer-in-charge of the United Nations Conference on

Trade and Development, the Deputy Director-General of the General Agreement on Tariffs and Trade, the Under-Secretary-General for Policy Coordination and Sustainable Development and the representative of the World Bank responded to questions raised during the exchange of views.

12. The President of the Council made some concluding remarks on the policy dialogue and discussion.

13. At the 11th meeting, on 28 June, the Council began its consideration of an agenda for development (agenda item 2).

14. The Secretary-General made a statement.

15. The President of the General Assembly also made a statement.

16. Statements were then made by the Permanent Representative of Algeria to the United Nations (on behalf of the States Members of the United Nations that are members of the Group of 77 and China); the Alternate Minister for Foreign Affairs of Greece (on behalf of the States Members of the United Nations that are members of the European Union); the Secretary of State (Asia-Pacific) of Canada; the Secretary-General of the Ministry of Foreign Affairs of France, the Administrator of the United States Agency for International Development; the Minister for Development of Denmark; the Permanent Representative of Senegal to the United Nations; the Permanent Representative of Mexico to the United Nations; the Minister for Foreign Affairs of Paraguay.

17. The Director-General of the Food and Agriculture Organization of the United Nations also made a statement.

18. At the 12th meeting, on 28 June, statements were made by the Deputy to the Minister for Foreign Economic Relations of Indonesia; the Deputy Secretary, Overseas Development Administration of the United Kingdom of Great Britain and Northern Ireland; the Minister of State for External Affairs of India; the Minister of State of Germany; the Under-Secretary of State, Ministry of Foreign Affairs of Poland; the Minister of Planning and Economic Development of Ethiopia; the Deputy Minister for Foreign Affairs of Romania; the Special Representative of Brazil to the high-level seg-

ment; the Deputy Foreign Minister for International Affairs of the Islamic Republic of Iran; the Permanent Representative of Sri Lanka to the United Nations; the Minister, Department of the Prime Minister of Malaysia; the Under-Secretary of State for Development Cooperation of Finland; the Secretary of State for Development Cooperation of Belgium; the Minister for Foreign Affairs of Costa Rica; the Planning Commissioner of the National Economic Planning Commission, Office of the President of Zimbabwe; the Under-Secretary of State of Sweden; the Secretary of the Economic Relations Division, Ministry of Finance of Bangladesh; the Deputy Prime Minister of the Republic of Croatia.

19. Statements were also made by the Director-General of the World Health Organization, the Director-General of the United Nations Educational, Scientific and Cultural Organization and the Director-General of the United Nations Industrial Development Organization.

20. At the 13th meeting, on 29 June, statements were made by the Chargé d'affaires of the Permanent Mission of Colombia to the United Nations; the Secretary of the General People's Committee for Economic and Commercial Affairs of the Libyan Arab Jamahiriya; the Minister of State of Ireland; the State Secretary of Norway; the State Secretary (Deputy Foreign Minister) of Slovenia; the Permanent Representative of China to the United Nations; the Special Assistant to the Prime Minister of Pakistan on Social Affairs; the Parliamentary Secretary, Office of the Prime Minister of the Bahamas; the First Deputy Minister for Foreign Affairs of Ukraine; the Deputy Minister for Foreign Affairs of Bulgaria; the Under-Secretary of State of Italy.

21. The observer for the European Community made a statement.

22. Statements were also made by the Administrator of the United Nations Development Programme, the Executive Director of the United Nations Children's Fund, the Executive Director of the United Nations Population Fund and the Executive Director of the World Food Programme.

23. The President of the Council made a statement to launch the dialogue, in which the Minister for Development of Denmark participated.

24. At the 14th meeting, on 29 June, statements were made by the Deputy Permanent Representative of Japan to the United Nations; the Deputy Minister for Foreign Affairs of the Russian Federation; the Permanent Representative of Austria to the United Nations; the Secretary of State for Cooperation, Ministry of Foreign Affairs of Portugal; the First Deputy Minister of the Ministry of Foreign Affairs and Permanent Representative of Cuba to the United Nations; the Permanent Representative of Venezuela to the United Nations; the Deputy Permanent Representative of Australia to the United Nations; the Ambassador Extraordinary and Plenipotentiary of Israel, the Permanent Representative of Jamaica to the United Nations, the Permanent Representative of Nepal to the United Nations; the Permanent Representative of Belarus to the United Nations; the Ambassador from the Ministry of Foreign Relations of the Former Yugoslav Republic of Macedonia; the Minister for Economic Affairs of Morocco; the Permanent Representative of the Republic of Korea to the United Nations; the Minister of Information and Minister of State of Jordan; the Minister for Economic Planning and Development of Swaziland; the Permanent Representative of Egypt to the United Nations; the Director of the Department for International Organizations of Switzerland.

25. Statements were made by the observers for the Latin American Economic System and the Organization of African Unity.

26. Statements were made by the Secretary-General of the International Civil Aviation Organization, the Deputy Director-General of the International Labour Organization and the Deputy High Commissioner for Refugees.

27. The representative of Greece made a statement.

28. At the 15th meeting, on 29 June, statements were made by the Deputy Permanent Representative of Madagascar to the United Nations; the Director General for International Organizations, Royal Foreign Office of Spain; the Permanent

Representative of Turkey to the United Nations; the Under-Secretary of Social Labour of Kuwait.

29. At the same meeting, the Council entered into a dialogue during which statements were made by the representatives of Angola, the United Kingdom of Great Britain and Northern Ireland, Germany, Benin, the Netherlands, Japan, Egypt, Senegal, China, Canada, France, Pakistan, Brazil, the United States of America, India, Australia and Nigeria and the observers for Algeria and the Netherlands.

30. Statements were also made by the representatives of the United Nations Development Programme and the World Bank.

31.The President of the Council made some concluding remarks.

B.   Conclusions of the high-level segment

32. At the 35th meeting, on 18 July, the President of the Council presented the summary and conclusions of the high-level segment (E/1994/109).

33. At the same meeting, statements were made by the representatives of the United States of America, the Russian Federation, Germany (on behalf of the States Members of the United Nations that are members of the European Union), Ukraine, China, Paraguay, the Libyan Arab Jamahiriya and Belarus and the observers for Algeria (on behalf of the States Members of the United Nations that are members of the Group of 77) and Kyrgyzstan.

34. The representative of the Food and Agriculture Organization of the United Nations also made a statement.

35. The President of the Council made some concluding remarks.

36. The principal elements emerging from the discussions are summarized below [see following page].

Summary and conclusions by Ambassador Richard Butler, AM, President of the Economic and Social Council

Summary

The state of affairs

"The following main relevant features of current global economic and social conditions were identified:

"While growth has resumed in the world economy overall, it is spread very unevenly and is by no means secure;

"A number of developing countries now play a key role in the world economy, yet the magnitude and spread of extreme poverty has increased greatly. Today, more than 1 billion people live in extreme poverty;

"Overall, the gap between developed and developing countries continues to widen. It reflects the marginalization of developing countries in respect of the main determinants of international trade, money, finance, technology, and information and communication flows;

"Notwithstanding stronger growth in some developed countries, unemployment rates remain alarmingly high;

"Integration/globalization in the global economy is now one of its fundamental pervasive features;

"Sustainable development needs to be pursued;

"Levels of official development assistance continue to decline. There is a crisis of official development assistance characterized by a stagnation, in some cases a reduction, in aid budgets, contrary to the target of 0.7 per cent of gross national product, as agreed;

"Globally, levels of direct private investment in developing countries are increasing, although such investment is spread unevenly and cannot, in many cases, be a substitute for official development assistance;

"Emergency assistance is now absorbing a significant proportion of the resources being made available to developing countries by the United Nations;

"An increasing portion of growth in world trade is being generated by some developing countries. This is positive for the global economy and points further towards the need to support growth in developing countries;

"The completion of the Uruguay Round of multilateral trade negotiations of the GATT and the creation of the World Trade Organization hold out the prospect of significant benefits to the world economy. While the benefits of the Uruguay Round should be equal to all, they could be uneven initially. They will depend, in part, on sound export-oriented policies. Their wider or complete realization requires the implementation of the transition arrangements for developing countries and the forging, as appropriate, of greater coherency between trade, monetary and finance policies, as well as the prevention and redress of unilateral actions of a protectionist nature;

"In the present decade, a considerable number of developing countries have implemented trade liberalization measures, such as reducing their tariff rates. This is a positive trend, which should be accompanied by similar measures on the part of developed countries where that has not already occurred;

"The debt burden remains a constraint on the development efforts of many developing countries, particularly in Africa and the least developed countries, which continue to experience severe debt-service difficulties. This situation continues to impede development efforts;

"Special attention needs to be given to the least developed countries and the most vulnerable groups. The continuing critical economic situation of Africa constitutes a failure of serious proportions in itself and in the global economy;

"The obstacles to economic and social development being experienced in the economies in transition are serious intrinsically and in global terms;

"The situation of women in the global economy, especially in poorer countries, is a cause for deep concern in human and social terms and constitutes a serious failure of utilization of a highly productive resource in economic terms.

Priorities

"In the debate on the theme 'An agenda for development', the following issues were identified as being basic to contemporary circumstances and/or needing to be addressed if a new agenda is to be implemented:

"The need for political agreement among all States to assign priority in policy, actions, and allocation of resources for global economic and social development – that is, for improving significantly the standard of life of the very considerable number of the world's people who live in developing countries. A new agenda must be action-oriented, based on a spirit of partnership, and give due attention to national specificities;

"This commitment would be based on recognition of both qualitative and quantitative goals, the need to distinguish between urgent and deep-seated tasks, and the fundamental importance of economic growth and of sustainable development;

"Recognition of the fundamental right to development, as stated in the Vienna Declaration adopted by the World Conference on Human Rights, and of the linkage between peace and development, and recognition that democracy, development and respect for human rights and fundamental freedoms are interdependent and mutually reinforcing;

"The importance of economic growth and social justice which includes the promotion of equality of opportunity for all members of society;

"The United Nations has a unique opportunity to act now on a new agenda for development. Present circumstances will not necessarily prevail for long. Failure to seize this opportunity could have widespread and deeply damaging effects because of the existence of conditions in the world economic and social situation which are global and interlocked;

"Development is a global issue. There is a need to recognize the diversity of the developing world and to strengthen differentiated and comprehensive approaches, as well as both North-South and South-South cooperation;

"It is essential that all relevant actors be involved in a new agenda – institutions of civil society, non-governmental organizations and the private sector, as well as Governments and international organizations. An agenda which is simply auto-suggestive will fail;

"A new agenda for development must be centred primarily on people. While recognizing the importance of overall economic development needs, action programmes must give appropriate priority to the education, health and welfare of people. Within this framework, institutions – both governmental and those of civil society – need to be strengthened;

"A concerted attack must be made on the grinding poverty that afflicts over 1 billion people. Action must be directed particularly towards the elimination of its underlying causes. Special attention must be given to the least developed countries and, in particular, to Africa;

"The status of women must be given particular attention. Women must be integrated into decision-making and mainstream economic activities. The economic and social return on investment in their education, health and welfare is greater than that on almost any other comparable investment;

"Among the constraints to development is rapid population growth. A new agenda should incorporate clear and effective population policies within the context of overall sustainable development;

"The issues of declining national official development assistance and the growing proportion of multilateral development funds being devoted to emergency rather than development purposes must be addressed;

"An agenda for development must consider the fundamental role of science and technology, particularly for developing countries. It should identify ways and means of improving and facilitating the access and transfer of technology to developing countries;

"External factors such as trade, debt, commodity prices, transfer of technology and financial flows are critical to the success or failure of the domestic efforts of developing countries;

"Regional economic integration is complementary to multilateralism. The process of regional integration should contribute towards an open trading system;

"Governments have a prime responsibility to ensure the framework conditions for development based on self-help efforts;

"It has become clear that United Nations machinery operates today in ways that are inadequate to the present challenge. There is no support for the establishment of new machinery but an insistence that the present machinery be made to function vastly more effectively than at present, particularly at Headquarters. At the field level, the resident coordinator system must continue to be strengthened;

"Action to make United Nations machinery operate more effectively should begin by identifying the areas of work in which the United Nations has a comparative advantage and shedding those areas in which it does not;

"A stronger role for the United Nations in development, including in the operational field, is needed. The role of the United Nations in relation to that of other actors also needs to be clarified. This would facilitate action-oriented recommendations by the Secretary-General for the United Nations system in the implementation of an agenda for development;

"There is considerable room for improvement in the relationship between the United Nations and the Bretton Woods institutions. The social dimensions of structural adjustment programmes also require further attention.

Conclusions

"The statements made during the high-level segment of the Economic and Social Council, the World Hearings on Development and further consultations with members of the Council, pointed towards issues of central priority for action on an agenda for development. Decisions on such action will be considered by the General Assembly.

"To facilitate that consideration, the Secretary-General will submit a further report on an agenda for development to the General Assembly at its forty-ninth session. I hope that, in formulating his report, he will take into account the priorities recorded in the present document.

"In addition, with respect to the activities of the United Nations development system, much was said in the Council about the need for greater clarity with respect to the comparative advantages of that system.

"In this context, I believe two basic considerations are relevant:

"The United Nations disposes directly of only a fraction of global resources relevant to development;

"At the same time, the United Nations has uniquely at its disposal the ability to build consensus for globally relevant political decisions. This is its central comparative advantage.

"If that advantage is exercised on the basis of an accurate analysis of relevant data, it should assist those who dispose of very significant resources to commit them in ways compatible with the priorities identified by the United Nations and thus join with the United Nations in the crucial enterprise of development.

INDEX

The numbers following the entries refer to paragraph numbers in the three reports that have been indexed. The letter "A" before the paragraph number refers to the "Note by the Secretary-General" reproduced on pages 5-15; the letter "B" refers to the "Report of the Secretary-General" reproduced on pages 17-82; and the letter "C" refers to the "Recommendations" of the Secretary-General, reproduced on pages 83-106. The documents in Section Two are not indexed.

UNITED NATIONS PUBLICATIONS OF RELATED INTEREST

THE FOLLOWING UN PUBLICATIONS MAY BE OBTAINED FROM THE ADDRESSES
INDICATED BELOW, OR AT YOUR LOCAL DISTRIBUTOR:

An Agenda for Peace
SECOND EDITION, 1995
BY BOUTROS BOUTROS-GHALI,
SECRETARY-GENERAL OF THE UNITED NATIONS
E.95.I.15   92-1-100555-8   155PP.

Building Peace and Development, 1994
ANNUAL REPORT OF THE WORK OF THE ORGANIZATION
BY BOUTROS BOUTROS-GHALI,
SECRETARY-GENERAL OF THE UNITED NATIONS
E.95.I.3   92-1-100541-8   299PP.

New Dimensions of Arms Regulations and Disarmament in the Post–Cold War Era
BY BOUTROS BOUTROS-GHALI,
SECRETARY-GENERAL OF THE UNITED NATIONS
E.93.IX.8   92-1-142192-6   53PP. $9.95

Basic Facts About the United Nations
E.93.I.2   92-1-100499-3   290PP. $5.00

Demographic Yearbook, Vol.44
B.94.XIII.1   92-1-051083-6   1992   823PP. $125.00

Disarmament—New Realities: Disarmament, Peace-Building and Global Security
E.93.IX.14   92-1-142199-3   397PP. $35.00

United Nations Disarmament Yearbook, Vol.18
E.94.IX.1   92-1-142204-3 1993   419PP. $50.00

Statistical Yearbook, 39th Edition
B.94.XVII.1 H   92-1-061159-4   1992/93   1,174PP. $110.00

Women: Challenges to the Year 2000
E.91.I.21   92-1-100458-6   96PP. $12.95

World Economic and Social Survey 1994
E.94.II.C.1   92-1-109128-4   308PP. $55.00

World Investment Report 1994—Transnational Corporations, Employment and the Work Place
E.94.II.A.14   92-1-104435-9   446PP. $45.00

Yearbook of the United Nations, Vol. 46
E.93.I.1   0-7923-2583-4   1992   1277PP. $150.00

* * *

THE UNITED NATIONS BLUE BOOKS SERIES

The United Nations and Apartheid, 1948-1994
E.95.I.7   92-1-100546-9   565PP. $29.95

The United Nations and Cambodia, 1991-1995
E.95.I.9   92-1-100548-5   360PP. $29.95

FORTHCOMING:
The United Nations and the Nuclear Non-Proliferation Treaty
The United Nations and El Salvador, 1990-1995
The United Nations and Mozambique, 1992-1995

UNITED NATIONS PUBLICATIONS
2 UNITED NATIONS PLAZA, ROOM DC2-853
NEW YORK, NY 10017
UNITED STATES OF AMERICA

UNITED NATIONS PUBLICATIONS
SALES OFFICE AND BOOKSHOP
CH-1211 GENEVA 10
SWITZERLAND